The Fantasy Factory
Lime Grove Studios, London

1915-1991

A HISTORY COMPILED BY
Jocelyn Lukins

FOR ROBIN H. WILLIAMS
1920-1941

07753594

ACKNOWLEDGMENTS

In compiling this history I gratefully acknowledge the assistance afforded by the study facilities of The British Film Institute, Stills Department and Library; The London Borough of Hammersmith and Fulham, Archives and Local History Centre and The Shepherd's Bush branch of their public library.

I am also very grateful for help given by Charles & Joan Blake of the Shepherd's Bush Local History Society; Brian Adams; Audrey Atterbury; Malcolm Dormer; Thelma Lister; Norma McCaw; Doug Pinchin; Dave Sandall, The Tony Hancock Society; Tony Smith; David Stone; and many others including the people who worked at Lime Grove some of whom I have had the priviledge of meeting and many whom I have got to know through their published comments on their time there, through their autobiographies and their biographers.

Published by Venta Books
14 Keith Grove
London W12 9EZ

Designed by Pep Reiff

Set by Cassandra Moulen

Printed by Bookmag, Inverness

First Published 1996 for The Shepherd's Bush Local History Society
© Jocelyn Lukins 1996 I.S.B.N.0 9510288 8X

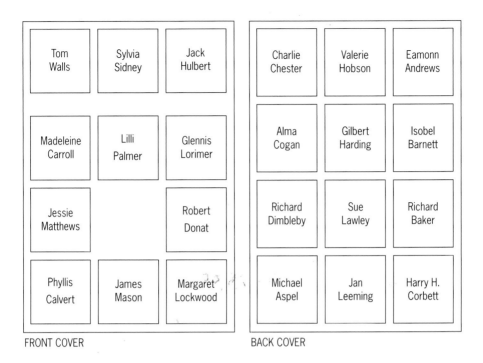

Tom Walls	Sylvia Sidney	Jack Hulbert		Charlie Chester	Valerie Hobson	Eamonn Andrews
Madeleine Carroll	Lilli Palmer	Glennis Lorimer		Alma Cogan	Gilbert Harding	Isobel Barnett
Jessie Matthews		Robert Donat		Richard Dimbleby	Sue Lawley	Richard Baker
Phyllis Calvert	James Mason	Margaret Lockwood		Michael Aspel	Jan Leeming	Harry H. Corbett

FRONT COVER   BACK COVER

The list of films and television shows is not meant to be comprehensive. The alternative film titles used for American release are not included. In most cases the date quoted is when the film was made rather than released.

SHEPHERD'S BUSH LOCAL HISTORY SOCIETY PUBLICATIONS

The Dickens Connection (£3.00)

Shepherd's Bush Markets and Traders (£2.00)

Around The Bush: A History Of Shepherd's Bush (£2.00)

Around The Bush: The War Years (£2.25)

For further information about The Shepherd's Bush Local History Society

Contact: The Secretary 22A Collingbourne Road London W12 0JQ

The Glass House 1915

1

1912 The Gaumont Film Co. acquired land in Lime Grove, Shepherd's Bush on which to build a film studio. The land had formerly belonged to the railway. I had always wondered how this large building, with its solid windowless exterior, had landed in this implied sylvan grove. However, until this block was built in 1915, the present Lime Grove only extended to this point where there were vast commercial premises. The extension beyond which linked with Goldhawk Road was known as Brookland Road. The building dwarfed the small domestic houses on either side of it and as time went on many of these were incorporated into the film, and later, the BBC Television Studios as the organisations spread.

Leon Gaumont, a pioneer cinematograph inventor, producer and exhibitor was French and the parent company was in Paris. The British branch, prior to the building of these studios, existed mainly as distributors of their French products which consisted mainly of newsreels and cartoons like:-

1914 STUDDY'S WAR STUDIES by G.E. Studdy of 'Bonzo' fame.
The newsreels were of the battlefields of the First World War, such as:-

1914 WITH OUR TERRITORIALS AT THE FRONT photographed by Geoffrey Malins.

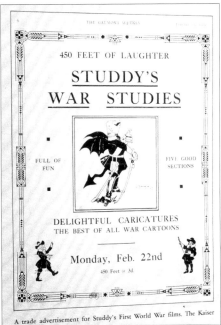

Gaumont put £30,000 into the construction of the film studio. A large sum to spend on a British studio which were usually converted skating rinks, tram sheds, gas works and factories until this custom built studio described by Clarence Winchester as, *The finest studio in Great Britain and the first building ever put up in this country solely for the production of films, the famous glass studio completed in 1914.* It was an ambitious project, four or five sets could be erected at once and frequently several films were in production side by side. There was a stage on the first floor and workshops and laboratories beneath. The all-glass daylight studio was 90 feet x 40 feet x 20 feet high with an end section 30 feet high. The "Glass House" was opened at the end of 1915. Although the finest in Britain it had no lot and was small by US standards.

The Gaumont Weekly 1915. Paul Babb and Gay Owen.

Ultus and The Grey Lady 1916. Gaumont British

1915 One of the most promising producers in England, George Pearson, joined Gaumont late in 1915 and the company embarked on a programme of feature film productions. Leon Gaumont wanted to make a series of films which would be as popular in Britain as his "Fantomas" series had been in France. George Pearson wrote and produced a series with well constructed plots with lots of punches per reel about a heroic adventurer called 'Ultus' (Latin for Avenger). Ultus was played by Aurele Sydney, of French descent and a native of Sydney Australia. He had joined the Gaumont Company in Paris before coming to England. He captured the audiences imagination and became an international success. His films were:-

March 1916 ULTUS THE MAN FROM THE DEAD with Marjorie Dunbar and J.L.V. Leigh.

October 1916 ULTUS AND THE GREY LADY with Mary Dibley and J.L.V. Leigh.

Also made in 1916 was:-

THE KUT RELIEF FORCE IN MESOPOTAMIA a 1,000 foot news film plus a more popular sounding series of Louis Wain cartoons was begun.

Two more 4-reel Ultus films were made:-

January 1917 ULTUS AND THE SECRET OF THE NIGHT with Mary Dibley and J.L.V. Leigh.

August 1917 ULTUS AND THE THREE BUTTON MYSTERY with Manora Thew followed by:-

1917 SALLY BISHOP starring Aurele Sydney and Peggy Hyland.

A 4-reel adaptation of E. Temple Thurston's novel. It was already found by 1917 that shooting by daylight was very limited in England. The glass walls were blacked out and "Westminster" arcs and Boardman "north light" lamps were moved in. The power supply was from the mains with a back-up motor generator. Cameras at that time were by 'Debrie' and film was processed in the laboratories on the premises. Gaumont made their own film stock which like other negative films at the time was orthochromatic, slow and quite insensitive to the red end of the spectrum so that red reproduced as black and heavy pale yellow Leichner No.5 make up was used.

Peggy Hyland. Hardie

The First Men On The Moon 1918. James Anderson Memorial Collection

The Passionate Adventure 1925. Claude McDonnell, Graham Cutts, Director, Alice Joyce and Marjorie Daw. Gaumont British

1918 The chief cameraman was at "the front" and George Pearson and Aurele Sydney left the company early in 1918 so that productions were not as ambitious for a time but under the direction of J.L.V Leigh they continued with:-

1918 THE "EVE" COMEDIES with Eileen Molyneux. Based on the drawings by Miss Fish in "The Tatler" magazine.
A one reeler.

KEY OF THE WORLD with Eric Harrison and Eileen Molyneux from a novel by Dorin Craig. Released in 1919.

PALLARD THE PUNTER with Heather Thatcher and J.L.V. Leigh and from a novel by Edgar Wallace released in 1919.

THE FIRST MEN ON THE MOON from a novel by H.G. Wells.

Heather Thatcher

Unlike the original scripts of George Pearson for the Ultus Films most scenarios at this time and in the future were taken from existing novels and current stage successes. At the end of the war escapism was in demand.

1921 Gareth Cundrey joined Gaumont as Editor in Charge of scenarios and the stories became more attuned to the wants of cinema audiences. Many box office successes followed in the 1920's. We are of course still in the silent era. At this time there was a decline in British films from 147 made in 1920 to 64 in 1923. The Americans had captured the market whilst Britain was set back by the War.

1925 THE PASSIONATE ADVENTURE with Lillian Hall-Davis and Clive Brook, directed by Graham Cutts.

1926 Maurice Elvey who had produced some very successful films was engaged by Gaumont and put in charge of production. His first film for them was:-

1926 MADEMOISELLE FROM ARMENTIERES with Estelle Brody and John Stuart with Victor Saville producing and Gareth Cundrey Scenario Editor. As a nostalgic and sanitised version of the 1914-18 War it was an immediate success with audiences and probably the most successful moneymaker produced in Great Britain until this date.

Mademoiselle From Armetieres 1926. John Stuart and The Concert Party. Gaumont British

Mademoiselle From Armetieres 1926. Victor Saville, Maurice Elvey and Cameraman. Gaumont British

1926 In March, the Gaumont British Picture Corporation registered a capital of £2,500,000. Onto the Board came persons representing distributors and cinema chains, to improve the distribution of the company's products. It was floated as a public company, "Gainsborough Pictures". Fox Film Corporation of America had a substantial holding in the Gaumont British Picture Corporation. The founding fathers of this large combine were Michael Balcon and Victor Saville, Producers. The President was Isadore Ostrer, a merchant banker of Polish extraction and one of the most powerful film magnates in Great Britain at the time, who gave financial backing and who owned a large chain of cinemas (187). Michael Balcon's Gainsborough Production Company also owned a studio in Islington, a converted powerhouse. This amalgamation was inspired by the impending British government's:-

1927 'British Cinematograph Film Act' stating that distributing firms and exhibitors must show a quota of up to 30% of British made films. So it was prudent for film companies to enlarge, amalgamate and reconstruct to improve their production and distribution facilities in order to take advantage of the quota legislation.

1926 At the end of the year the studio was closed to be enlarged and improved at a further reputed cost of £25,000.

The first production after the refurbishment was:-

1926 THE ARCADIANS a silent film version of the musical comedy. Despite the same winning combination as in the previous production, Victor Saville and Gareth Cundry, this was a flop.

John Stuart. *Picturegoer*   Estelle Brody. *Picturegoer*

8

Mabel Poulton, whose Cockney accent made her a victim of the talkies. *Picturegoer*

Benita Hume. *Dorothy Wilding*

The Flight Commander 1927. *Gaumont British*

Production continued with:-

1927 HINDLE WAKES with Estelle Brody and John Stuart. Direction by Maurice Elvey and camerawork by Basil Emmett and Percy Strong. The play by Stanley Houghton had a Lancashire setting and Elvey had previously filmed it in 1918. There were mill interiors and the Blackpool pleasure gardens. It told the story of a Lancashire mill girl who spends a week at Blackpool with the boss's son but refuses to marry him.

1927 ROSES OF PICARDY with Lilian Hall-Davis and John Stuart, from the novel by R.H. Mottram.

THE SPANISH FARM with Lilian Hall-Davis and John Stuart.

THE GLAD EYE with Estelle Brody and John Stuart from a stage comedy.

THE FLIGHT COMMANDER with Estelle Brody and John Stuart.

For this film a whole Chinese village was built at Hendon for bombardment scenes. The aerial thrills were provided by Sir Alan Cobham. There being no lot at Shepherd's Bush, location work and large sets had to be shot elsewhere.

1927 QUINNEYS with Alma Taylor and John Longdon from a novel by Horace Vachell, concerning a family of antique dealers.

1928 MADEMOISELLE PARLEY VOO

PALAIS DE DANCE with John Longdon and Mable Poulton. All these productions directed by Maurice Elvey were a moderate success and some were hits.

1928 THE PHYSICIAN with Miles Mander and Elga Brink was made as a joint Anglo-German production resulting from recent mergers.

Renate Muller. Film Weekly

John Stuart. Picturegoer

Hindle Wakes 1931, Belle Crystall, Edmund Gwenn and Sybil Thorndike. Gaumont British

Belle Chrystall. Gaumont British

Edmund Gwenn. Gaumont British

11

1929 Gaumont British owned 287 cinemas at this time.

1929 Brought the introduction of the talkies and further changes. The glass wall was made solid for sound proofing purposes and the studios became the largest sound studios in Europe. Michael Balcon was Head of Studio Production at Lime Grove and enlisted German technicians. Some of the first sound productions were:-

1929 HIGH TREASON with Benita Hume and directed by Maurice Elvey was remade in sound. It was a story set forward in time until 1940 when women unite to prevent the Second World War. There was a Channel Tunnel and they had audio visual telephones.

1931 THE GHOST TRAIN with Jack Hulbert, Cicely Courtneidge and Ann Todd, directed by Walter Forde, and produced by Michael Balcon. Made again 10 years later by Gainsborough, the story was adapted from a successful stage play by Arnold Ridley.

1931 SUNSHINE SUSIE with Jack Hulbert, Renate Muller and Owen Nares. Directed by Victor Saville, it was a comedy set in Vienna where a banker pretends to be a clerk to court a typist.

1931 HINDLE WAKES with Belle Crystall, John Stuart, Edmund Gwenn and Sybil Thorndike. A third version of this story, directed by Victor Saville. Arthur Crabtree made this film about class distinction again in 1952.

1931 THE CALENDAR with Herbert Marshall, Edna Best, Alfred Drayton, Anne Grey and Nigel Bruce. This racecourse melodrama by Edgar Wallace was directed by T. Hayes Hunter. It was made again by Gainsborough in 1948 with Greta Gynt and John McCallum.

Jack Hulbert and Cicely Courtneidge. Gainsborough.

The Calendar 1931. Herbert Marshall, Edna Best, and Anne Grey. Gaumont British

The Calendar 1931. Herbert Marshall and Edna Best, meeting at Beaconsfield. Sasha Ltd

13

Rome Express 1932. Walter and Cully Forde and stars. Gaumont British

1929-1932 ROME EXPRESS with Conrad Veidt and Gordon Harker, Directed by Walter Forde. This was the prototype train thriller from which THE LADY VANISHES and MURDER ON THE ORIENT EXPRESS later derived. Thieves and blackmail victims are among the passengers on a Wagon-Lits train. It was remade in 1948 by MGM as SLEEPING CAR TO TRIESTE. Production of this film was interrupted by a major refurbishment costing £250,000. Here are two contemporary accounts of the improved studios.

1932 *Gaumont had big ideas which they have embodied in a new studio opened in the summer of 1932 on the site of the old 'Glass House'. It is a huge, modern, white faced block, its flat roof towering 90 feet above the pavement. There are five production stages; dressing room accommodation for 600 artists; stars dressing rooms, the last word in comfort and decoration; laboratories with a minimum output capacity of 2,000,000 feet a week; three private theatres; an orchestration room; nine film vaults; a 600 seater restaurant; plasterers and carpenters shops; property rooms; monitor and recording rooms; all the paraphernalia of the last word in modern film studios is to be found at the Gaumont British studios in Lime Grove. They spent nearly half a million pounds on the studios but still were not content. Even now more floors and extra buildings are being added. The production of four films simultaneously will shortly be a simple matter. THE WORLD FILM ENCYCLOPEDIA Editor Clarence Winchester 1933.*

The flat roof was also used for outdoor shooting.

1.7.1932 In The West London Observer appeared this account of the opening.

Rome Express 1932. Walter Forde. Gaumont British

Rome Express 1932. A station built in the studio. Gaumont British

The Shepherd's Bush Studios of Gaumont British Picture Corporation. Building on left opened in 1932. Centre portion added in 1927. Building on right completed in 1933 stands on the sight of the original 1915 glasshouse.

This huge building was opened on Wednesday afternoon. The ceremony was viewed by dense crowds with several Gaumont stars present. The Chairman, Isadore Ostrer, was presented with souvenier gifts. This is the largest, best-equipped film studio in the country with two acres of studios, the largest 86' wide and 136' long. There are 500 dressing rooms, numerous laboratories and technical rooms and the offices occupy three floors. The first film to be made is ROME EXPRESS now in course of production in one of the large studios. In fact there were 49 dressing rooms!

A Stars Dressing Room 1933. Picture Show

1932 I WAS A SPY with Madeleine Carroll, Conrad Veidt, Herbert Marshall, Gerald du Maurier, and Edmund Gwenn. Directed by Victor Saville.

This was a first world war spy drama based on a true episode in the life of Marthe Knockhaert. She was a Belgium agent working as a nurse in a hospital behind German lines Madeleine Carroll met Marthe and some of the film was shot on location in Belgium. Back at Shepherd's Bush Madeleine Carroll said, *Just as the trip to the front with Herr Junge made me think of the futility of nations fighting, so my work in the studio with Conrad Veidt has confirmed my earlier thoughts. Here is a splendid man, a great artist and a gentleman. He is popular with the Englishmen in the cast – yet they were fighting on opposite sides during the War and presumably, 'hating' one another! Isn't it all stupid? Veidt and the rest of us were discussing the film between shots. We have decided it gives a very fair view on both sides.* Alfred Junge was Art Director. He rebuilt the interior of the Palace Hotel Brussels at Lime Grove for the film.

Jessie Matthews, publicity still 1934. Gaumont British

The Good Companions 1933. Sandy Bay Pavilion built at the studios. Gaumont British

The Good Companions 1933. Gaumont British

19

1932 Victor Saville, who at 35 was the studios ace director and a master of the romantic style was watching the final rushes of There Goes The Bride in the private projection room at Lime Grove. It was being made by Michael Balcon at Beaconsfield Studios. The star was Jessie Matthews and Victor Saville realised he had found the actress he had been searching for to play the Susie Dean character in J.B. Priestley's:-

9.12.32 THE GOOD COMPANIONS However Albert de Courville was about to start shooting.

9.10.32 MIDSHIPMAID a musical comedy with Jessie Matthews. There was a war between the two directors and the result was that both films were shot simultaneously at Shepherd's Bush. Jessie Matthews was on the set at 6.30 am in the morning and she was still working at 3.00 am the following morning, after working 21 hours. On one occasion the sound man asked her if she could do something about her stomach rumbles as the microphone was picking them up *I sure can* she replied *I need some food. How about it? Don't start getting temperamental and trying to behave like a movie star* said de Courville. *You've only made three films.* She spent the autumn of 1932 racing between the two film sets at Shepherd's Bush and driving to her home at Hampton in the small hours. One night, exhausted, she fell asleep with her head against the horn and woke the neighbourhood. The one pleasant memory of MIDSHIPMAID for her was working with a charming, good looking young actor, John Mills, making his first film.

Victor Saville who directed THE GOOD COMPANIONS was a much more sympathetic character. Jessie Matthews was insecure, felt unsure of herself in films and wished to return to the theatre. Victor Saville said *Just look the camera straight in the eye and say to yourself, I am beautiful, I am beautiful and you will be.*

She was afterwards seen walking around Lime Grove silently mouthing these lines. Cast opposite her was John Geilgud with whom she shared a sense of the ridiculous at enacting intimate love scenes surrounded by a circle of technicians.

Meanwhile her first film THERE GOES THE BRIDE opened and she was hailed as,

A sparkling addition to the world's great film stars – London Evening News

A brilliantly original cinema star – The Daily Mail

She is going to be the biggest star name in this country – C.A. Lejeune.

1933 Hollywood offers were made. THE GOOD COMPANIONS was chosen as the first talkie to be shown before Queen Mary and King George V at a charity matinee at the New Victoria cinema. As she had recently been the subject of a notorious divorce case, Jessie Matthews could not be presented but Victor Saville and J.B. Priestley were. However, Queen Mary spotting her in the audience, gave her a warm smile.

1933 THE GOOD COMPANIONS with John Geilgud, Edmund Gwenn, Max Miller and Jack Hawkins was hailed as a tremendous success and Michael Balcon signed Jessie Matthews on a long contract. He said of her, *she dances like an angel.* She became a great asset to the studio and their first international star.

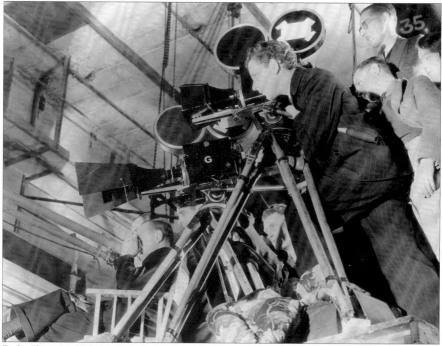

The Good Companions 1933. Victor Saville directing, Bernard Knowles on camera, with Gordon Lang and Jack Whitehead. Gaumont British

The Good Companions 1933. Gaumont British

The Good Companions 1933. Station scene. Gaumont British

John Gielgud 1933. Gaumont British

The Good Companions. Station scene in the studio. Gaumont British

22

It's Love Again 1936. A journalist interviews Jessie whilst her hairdresser works. Also in the film Robert Hale, father-in-law and Sara Allgood. Gaumont British

It's Love Again 1936. Sonnie Hale and Jessie Matthews. Gaumont British

The Odeon, Weston-super-mare opened in 1935. The Author's local. The Nevitsky Collection

1933 The quota system by which every cinema wanting to show an American film was obliged to show a British film in the same programme made film studios a hive of activity at this time. A shooting schedule of a film could be as little as eight days and it led to a lot of inferior B pictures, 'quota quickies' being produced. However, the Gainsborough label used on films made at Lime Grove from 1931 was attached to some excellent productions.

1933 Oscar Deutsch's circuit of 26 ODEON theatres with their distinctive style and Doulton 'Carrara' frontages were incorporated into the company and Gaumont British had the eighth largest cinema circuit.

There followed a string of Jessie Matthews films at Lime Grove. Her 'throbby' voice and magnificent legs were exploited to the full.

9.11.1933 WALTZES FROM VIENNA a costumed operetta based on the stage musical The Great Waltz with Edmund Gwenn as Johann Strauss. It was directed by Alfred Hitchcock who said, *I hate this sort of thing. Melodrama is the only thing I can do.*

He was to look back on this later as the worst of his films. *My lowest ebb.* Miss Matthews and her director did not hit it off. Success had gone to her head and they both wanted to be 'the star'. Jessie Matthews too thought the film *perfectly dreadful* but John Russell Taylor, Alfred Hitchcock's biographer feels the film *is actually rather charming.*

During this film the cameraman was Glen Williams, an American and the make up man was German, so they were a very cosmopolitan lot at Lime Grove in those days. Her next film was EVERGREEN which she had made a success in the theatre. Here a young actress pretends to be her sixty year old actress mother.

53-17b

First A Girl 1935. *Gaumont British*

Fred Astaire, then on the London stage, was talked of as her co-star but after only one film RKO had signed him and refused to release him.

The shooting of EVERGREEN was to begin on December 27th 1933, but after only an hour Jessie Matthews collapsed on the set at Shepherd's Bush she had been rushed to a Kensington nursing home suffering from nervous exhaustion only 12 days previously. The film progressed very carefully. A day bed was built for her on the set and a nurse was in attendance to see she rested between shots.

12.1933 EVERGREEN with Sonnie Hale and Betty Balfour. Directed by Victor Saville. Screenplay by Emlyn Williams. Music by Rodgers and Hart. "Dancing on the Ceiling", a long solo dance she rehearsed in the morning and it was shot in the afternoon. "When You Get a Little Springtime in your Heart" and "Over My Shoulder" were two more numbers which will always be associated with her.

1934 The film was finished in March and released later that year. Whilst it was being made it was decided to make EVENSONG with Evelyn Laye, an established musical comedy star and formerly married to Sonnie Hale, now married to Jessie Matthews. Evelyn Laye had sued Jessie Matthews in a very public divorce suit in 1929 and one night had stuck her hatpin into Jessie's tyres when she had found her car parked outside her husband's flat! Michael Balcon was apprehensive at having the two of them in the same studio. Michael Balcon asked Jessie Matthews if the *situation would disturb her?* She was very gracious, *of course I have no objection* she said. However when the costume designer, Lionel Burleigh travelled up in the lift with both of them one day he said *they stood in freezing silence on each side of me the whole journey.* In company they acknowledged one another but ignored each other when passing in one of the many corridors.

1934 EVERGREEN when released was a great success both sides of the Atlantic.

Princess Personality herself. She can sing, she can dance, she can act, she can look, she has charm, youth, beauty and a million dollars worth of magnetism, this is not a prediction, this is a promise, Jessie Matthews will be one of the biggest box office bets in America within the next six months 'Variety'.

Fred Astaire at about the same time received nothing like this praise.

Can't sing, can't act, can dance a little and yet it was his talents that stood the test of time.

Jessie Matthews had the world at her feet but her personal life wasn't happy. She had lost a son in 1935, her marriage to Sonnie Hale was shakey and she adopted a daughter to try and cement it.

Evensong 1934. Directed by Victor Saville. Gaumont British

It's Love Again 1936. The spangled cat suit. Gaumont British

First A Girl 1935. Jessie Matthews & Sonnie Hale. Gaumont British

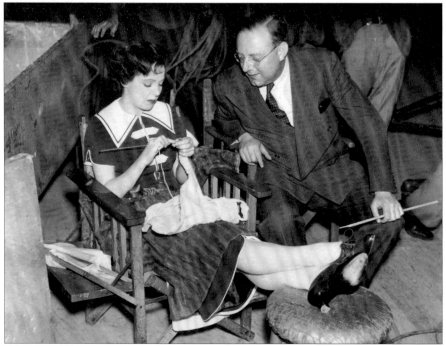

It's Love Again 1936. Jessie explains the art of knitting to Victor Saville. Gaumont British

1934 In September she had signed a new £50,000 contract with Gaumont British to make two films a year for three years. Hollywood had made many offers, one was from RKO to co-star with Fred Astaire but she stayed with Gaumont British.

1935 In April she returned after a break of make FIRST A GIRL (the original title 'Victor Victoria' was retained when Julie Andrews re-made it in 1982). The changed title was to celebrate the star's famous daughter. Her co-star was her husband Sonnie Hale. In one scene Jessie sang in a 40' bird cage which even Shepherd's Bush studios couldn't accommodate and it had to be built in the fields at Northolt. It was shot at night against a blackened sky and Jessie sat on her perch dressed only in sequins and feathers from 2-5 am in the early morning. She hated heights and it rained and was chilly despite the 140 arc lamps. This scene was chosen for the Royal Variety Performance before George V and Queen Mary, but was banned in the United States.

1936 IT'S LOVE AGAIN with Robert Young, who came from the US to be her co-star. Music by Irving Berlin who said *America worships her* when he visited the UK. In the film she wore a spangled cat suit which shocked some but Victor Saville, the Director, said *We have got to sell that body.* On one occasion she rode a camel into the studio at Shepherd's Bush.

First A Girl 1935. Gaumont British

It's Love Again 1936. Gaumont British

1936 Victor Saville left Gaumont British due to a salary dispute. Sonnie Hale became the director of her next film but he was so tyranical that the star was put under great strain. The studio closed in the middle of the shooting of HEAD OVER HEELS with Robert Flemyng for financial reasons.

When the shooting was due to restart in August 1936 the star was in a nursing home suffering from nervous exhaustion. She had her appendix removed, and developed a thrombosis in her leg, a tragedy for a dancer. She told her doctor *If I don't dance, I don't live.*

7.12.36 When she returned to Shepherd's Bush to finish HEAD OVER HEELS the 500 Gaumont British employees presented her with a bouquet, the card said, *It's grand to have you back.* Each had contributed one penny. She had frequent rests in her dressing room and left the studio at 5.00 pm.

The film was finished and Edward VIII had abdicated.

This was a bad time for the British film industry. Gaumont British was in debt to £100,000 on the previous year's trading. Over expansion produced more films than the circuits could carry. Gaumont British Distributors folded. Michael Balcon said, *To remain solvent it is not enough to make good and successful films.*

26.2.1937 Lime Grove studios was closed and the 500 employees were out of work.

Jessie Matthews' next films were made at Pinewood with Sonnie Hale, *a pitiably amateurish director* Graham Greene.

March 1938 Evelyn Bosman, Jessie's secretary continued to work at Lime Grove dealing with her stacks of fan mail which represented 70% of the mail received there.

Sonnie Hale's contract expired and Jessie Matthew's contract was due to expire in September 1938 when she made one last film, a slapstick comedy written by Sonnie Hale, at Pinewood.

1938 CLIMBING HIGH with Michael Redgrave. Directed by Carol Reed.

The film had a stormy passage. At one point, Michael Redgrave, making his third film asked if he must speak, *this ghastly musical comedy dialogue? My husband wrote that ghastly dialogue,* retorted Jessie. Carol Reed still a relatively young and inexperienced director making the film as he needed the work, said to Jessie Matthews one morning as she arrived on the set, *Matthews when you take off that I'm so beautiful look we might start shooting.* Jessie said, *How dare you! It took Victor Saville five years to get that look on my face. I used to sidle onto the set looking like a half drowned cat until I learned not to be frighted by people like you.* The relationship took a different turn when she playfully pushed a custard pie into his face one day. The film had a lukewarm reception.

Jessie did return to Lime Grove in 1944 and 1961. There had been some very good and successful films, Jessie Matthews was their star vehicle but there was a lot else going on in the thirties. A film they could be proud of was:-

1934 JEW SUSS with Conrad Veidt, Benita Hume, Gerald du Maurier and Pamela Ostrer. Produced by Michael Balcon and directed by Lothar Mendes. It was an historical satire on the pointlessness of race discrimination made in answer to the Nazi oppression in Germany at the time. The proceeds of the premiere were donated to the Fund for Distressed Miners. One of the cameramen was Roy Kellino, who later married Pamela Ostrer, who later still became Mrs James Mason.

Jew Suss 1934. Conrad Veidt and Benita Hume. Gaumont British

Jew Suss, Pamela Ostrer, aged 17.　　　*Gordon Harker. Picturegoer*

In a lighter vein, Michael Balcon produced many comedies.

1931 THE SPORT OF KINGS with Leslie Henson and Gordon Harker. Directed by Victor Saville. This adaptation of an established stage favourite was the first of these screen farces.

1932 JACK'S THE BOY with Jack Hulbert and Cicely Courtneidge. Directed by Walter Forde. Where Jack as a Policeman rounds up a smash and grab gang and sang his hit, 'The Flies Crawled up the Window'. It was shown before Queen Mary at the New Gallery Cinema, in March 1933.

1932 LOVE ON WHEELS with Jack Hulbert, Gordon Harker and Edmund Gwenn. Directed by Victor Saville. 'A Zippy Little Comedy', set in a department store. Selfridges was used as a setting.

1933 IT'S A BOY with Leslie Henson, Edward Everett Horton and Robertson Hare. Directed by Tim Whelan. 'A Hilarious Comedy' adapted from a stage success where a blackmailer claims to be the bridegroom's son on the eve of the wedding.

1934 BULLDOG JACK with Jack Hulbert, Ralph Richardson, Fay Wray and Claude Hulbert. Directed by Walter Forde. Here Jack poses as Bulldog Drummond in a comedy thriller with exciting scenes in the London underground and the British Museum.

1934 JACK AHOY with Nancy O'Neill and Alfred Drayton. Directed by Walter Forde. Where Jack is a naval rating routing bandits.

Love On Wheels 1932. Mobile units outside Selfridges. Gainsborough

33

Jack's The Boy 1932. A London street complete with bus in the studio. Gainsborough

Love On Wheels 1932. Jack Hulbert and Gordon Harker in drag. Gainsborough

A Cup Of Kindness 1934. Ralph Lynn and Robertson Hare. Gainsborough

Claude Hulbert

Diana Churchill. Gaumont British

Clarence Winchester describes how, *one Saturday night at Shepherd's Bush, the biggest sound stage was occupied by a complete ship used in Jack Ahoy. By the following Monday morning the whole ship had been dismantled and a complete street had taken its place for Waltzes from Vienna.*

1934 THE CAMELS ARE COMING with Jack Hulbert and Anna Lee. Directed by Tim Whelan.
Where Jack in the Camel Corp. catches Egyptian drug smugglers.

1936 JACK OF ALL TRADES with Jack Hulbert, Gina Malo and Robertson Hare. Directed by Jack Hulbert, at Islington.
Where Jack as a con man talks his way into a top job.
Jack Hulbert spent eight years in films. These popular musical comedies were complemented with song and dance numbers by Jack and partners. It was said of him, *His abounding energy and high spirits are never monotonous or wearisome* E.V. Lucas 'Punch'.

Fay Wray. Capitol

Cicely Courtnedge, Mrs Jack Hulbert made musical comedies on her own with Gainsborough including SOLDIERS OF THE KING 1933, AUNT SALLY 1933 and EVERYBODY DANCE 1936.

Popular at the time but dated now, these films are not often seen today. The performers who have stood the test of time a little better are the creators of the Alwych Farce, Tom Walls, Ralph Lynn and Robertson Hare. They were all from plays written by Ben Travers who adapted the scripts for the films and Tom Walls directed them all.

Anna Lee. Gaumont British

1934 A CUP OF KINDNESS with Claude Hulbert and Dorothy Hyson.

1935 FOREIGN AFFAIRS with Diana Churchill and Marie Lohr.

1935 FIGHTING STOCK with Lesley Waring and Marie Lohr.

1936 POT LUCK with Diana Churchill (daughter of Winston) and Martita Hunt.

Leslie Henson

Good Morning Boys 1937. Graham Moffatt and Will Hay. Gainsborough

Graham Moffatt

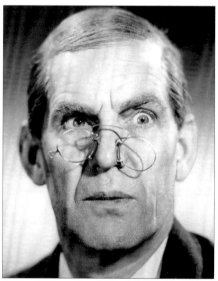

Will Hay. Gainsborough

Michael Balcon signed another popular comedian, peculiarly English, Will Hay, often seen in the guise of a seedy schoolmaster and very often with his companions, an artful old man, Moore Marriott and an equally artful fat boy, Graham Moffatt, who was a local boy from Shepherd's Bush. Graham was in Mr Bottle's class at Ellerslie Road School and went to the scout group in St. Stephens Church Hall. He got a job as a messenger at Lime Grove studios, was 'discovered' by Tom Walls and became an actor. The impertinent fat boy of the Will Hay comedies and many more films made at Lime Grove and Islington. He was sixteen when he appeared in Where There's a Will.

Will Hay made a number of films with Gainsborough, at Shepherd's Bush and Islington before the War, but later ones were made at Ealing. The Gainsborough Studios at Shepherd's Bush and Islington were interchangeable as venues before the War.

1935 BOYS WILL BE BOYS with Gordon Harker and Jimmy Hanley. Directed by William Beaudine.

1936 WHERE THERE'S A WILL with Hartley Power and Graham Moffatt. Directed by William Beaudine.

1936 WINDBAG THE SAILOR with Moore Marriott and Graham Moffatt. Directed by William Beaudine

1937 GOOD MORNING BOYS with Lilli Palmer and Graham Moffatt. Directed by Marcel Varnel it was made at the Islington Studios.

1937 OH MR PORTER with Moore Marriott and Graham Moffatt. Directed by Marcel Varnel.

1938 CONVICT 99 with Moore Marriot and Graham Moffat. Directed by Marcel Varnel.

1938 OLD BONES OF THE RIVER with Moore Marriot and Graham Moffat. Directed by Marcel Varnel.

1939 ASK A POLICEMAN with Moore Marriott and Graham Moffatt. Directed by Marcel Varnel. Marcel Varnel was the foremost comedy director.

Gainsborough

Secret Agent 1936. Madeleine Carroll, Peter Lorre, Alfred Hitchcock and Robert Young. Gainsborough

Peter Lorre

John Loder. Picturegoer

1933 Michael Balcon signed an innovative young director, Alfred Hitchcock but the first film he made at Gaumont was the ill fated WALTZES FROM VIENNA. A mild, romantic comedy and not at all his style. His next film under Ivor Montague was:-
1934 THE MAN WHO KNEW TOO MUCH with Leslie Banks, Peter Lorre and Nova Pibeam. There were memorable Hitchcockian sequences, one of which was set in the Albert Hall. This film re-established his reputation and he remade it for Paramount in 1956, but it is not considered as good a version.

Alfred Hitchcock

The next film has become a classic and although it has been filmed twice since in 1959 and 1978 this remains the greatest version.
1935 THE THIRTY NINE STEPS with Robert Donat and Madeleine Carroll.
It owed little to the original John Buchan novel, but the adaptation was good and Hitchcock's interpretation brilliant. The sequence of photographs show how much of the film was shot in the studio. A Scottish moor was built, complete with 62 sheep. A complete Scottish village was built at Welwyn. Robert Donat and Madeleine Carroll who made such a good team in the film apparently hated one another. At first they spent many sequences handcuffed together and Alfred Hitchcock who had a reputation for practical joking at the expense of his stars, on one occasion accidentally on purpose lost the key to the handcuffs for the whole day's shooting! The contratemps doesn't show. The scenes come over as both comic and erotic and the film has been described as *humorous, exciting, dramatic, entertaining, pictorial, vivid and novel, told with a fine sense of character and a keen grasp of the cinematic idea* S.W. Carroll.

The 39 Steps 1935. The original sketch of the Bridge and finished set. Gainsborough

The 39 Steps 1935. Madeleine Carroll and Robert Donat being directed by Alfred Hitchcock. Gainsborough

The 39 Steps 1935. The Scottish Moors in Shepherd's Bush. Gainsborough

Sabotage 1936. Alfred Hitchcock and John Loder on location. Gainsborough

Sabotage 1936. Alfred Hitchcock and Oscar Homolka. Gainsborough

43

Hitch's next film was:-

1936 SABOTAGE with Oscar Homolka, Sylvia Sidney and John Loder. From a story by Joseph Conrad, *it had a splendid brooding melodramatic atmosphere.* Central London was rebuilt at Shepperton from a few extras and some large photographic murals.

For the sequence when a bomb explodes on a London tram, Hitchcock had a tram line laid from Lime Grove to White City at a cost of £3,000 for the day's shoot. Ivor Montague thought the expense unjustified but Hitch got his way.

1936 THE SECRET AGENT with John Geilgud, Robert Young, Madeleine Carroll and Peter Lorre was another spy story, Ashenden by Somerset Maugham.

1937 YOUNG AND INNOCENT with Derrick de Marney and Nova Pilbeam, it was shot at Lime Grove and Pinewood. This was Hitchcock's favourite British film.

Although Hitchcock's last film in England was made by Gainsborough at their Islington studios, while Lime Grove was shut down, it is important enough to bear mention.

1938 THE LADY VANISHES with Michael Redgrave and Margaret Lockwood. Hitchcock was second choice as director, it was lucky for us he got the job as it has been said of Hitch's version, *directed with such skill and velocity that it has come to represent the very quintessence of screen suspense* Pauline Kael.

Dame May Whitty who played the vanishing lady was subjected to Hitchcock's rather harsh way of getting the best performances out of his stars. In the middle of her first scene he shouted *Stop! That's terrible.* The angry stars would then give the performance of their lives. Hitch told Edward Black, *Break 'em down right at the start, its much the best way.* Instead of calling 'Action' he had the habit of throwing a piece of china down!

Sabotage 1936. Sylvia Sidney and Oscar Homolka. Gainsborough

Secret Agent 1936. Percy Marmont, John Gielgud and The Swiss Alps at Shepherd's Bush. Gainsborough

Secret Agent 1936. Alfred Hitchcock directing Robert Young. Gainsborough

45

It was in this film that Basil Radford and Naunton Wayne made their first appearance as 'Charters and Caldicott', two very English cricket enthusiasts who are so absorbed in their Test Match cricket scores that anything else, like the dramatic events in this film, become quite secondary. The characters created by the writers, Launder and Gilliat, Hitchcock and the two actors were recreated in later films. This was Michael Redgrave's first starring role. The film was full of talent.

1940 Alfred Hitchcock left for a successful career in Hollywood. Peter Lorre of Hungarian Jewish descent, one of the screen's best known villains, also left about this time. There has always been a drift of actors and directors across the Atlantic.

'What days' it must have been at Lime Grove in the thirties, Jessie Matthews, and Evelyn Laye, rubbing shoulders with

John Mills

Alfred Hitchcock and Peter Lorre, Will Hay and Robert Donat, Jack and Claude Hulbert. There was another young man who did a series of films then, John Mills.

1932 After his debut with Jessie Matthews in MIDSHIPMAID, John Mills made many films at Lime Grove. He speaks in his biography of the studio in the early days being like *a Turkish bath* which was necessary as because of the slowness of the film stock a battery of arc lamps was needed. His first ever scene was at the piano surrounded by a group of sailors and Jessie Matthews and he had to sing a verse and chorus straight off. Despite his nervousness they printed 'take one'. He hadn't planned a career in films, but went straight on to make at Lime Grove:-

1933 BRITANNIA OF BILLINGSGATE with Violet Loraine, Gordon Harker and Kay Hammond. Directed by Walter Forde.

Glennis Lorrimer, who was the 'Gainsborough Lady' also appeared. The story told of a Billingsgate fried fish shop owner who became a film star and how the sudden wealth broke her family apart. Violet Loraine was praised for her portrayal of Britannia.

John Mills did want the title role in:-

1935 BROWN ON RESOLUTION with Betty Balfour and Jimmy Hanley from a story by C.S. Forester.

He went for an interview at Lime Grove with the director, Walter and his wife Cully Forde, and was turned down as *he didn't look like a sailor*. He hired a uniform from Bermans and presented himself at Forde's office again next day and wasn't recognised. He got the part for his *colossal nerve*, and has been playing sailors ever since. At the time this film was intended to be the largest and most expensive production ever tackled by a British studio. A small rocky island off Falmouth was bought for location work. It was a 1914 War story, the Admiralty approved the script and co-operated with a supply of warships and men. The location shots were directed by Anthony Asquith, son of the Prime Minister. It is about a single British sailor who holds a German raider at bay from a rocky island. 'Variety' called it, *A milestone in British pictures*. King George V and Queen Mary requested a private showing. The rave notices gave John Mills star status and he signed a two year contract with Gaumont British. The film was re-named Forever England and the story re-used in Sailor of The King in 1953.

Britannia of Billingsgate 1933. Piccadilly & Billingsgate market reconstructed at Shepherd's Bush.

Britannia of Billingsgate 1933. The eiderdowns are sound mufflers.

47

Constructing Piccadilly Circus in the workshops. Gainsborough

Gordon Harker. Gainsborough

Violet Loraine. Gainsborough

Brown on Resolution 1935. Walter and Cully Forde on location.
Gainsborough

48

Brown on Resolution 1935 with John Mills. Gainsborough

Ships engine room in the studio.

Britannia of Billingsgate 1933. Lighting platform and orchestra. Gainsborough

John Mills spoke of the following films as being *instantly forgettable*.

1935 DOCTOR'S ORDERS with Leslie Fuller.

CAR OF DREAMS with Greta Mosheim and Robertson Hare.

1936 BAD BLOOD with Lilli Palmer, mainly shot on location around Marseilles and Paris.

1936 O.H.M.S. with Anna Lee and Wallace Ford. Directed by Raoul Walsh.

1936 TUDOR ROSE with Nova Pilbeam and Cedric Hardwicke. Directed by Robert Stevenson. The story of Lady Jane Grey, this film was labelled *a modestly made historical drama*. John Mills returned to Lime Grove later to make more memorable films.

Tudor Rose 1936. Nova Pilbeam aged 16. Gainsborough

Orders is Orders 1933. Cyril Maude. Gainsborough

Me and Marlborough 1936. Cicely Courtneidge. Gainsborough

Sleeping Car 1933. Ivor Novello. Gainsborough

Ivor Novello and Madeleine Carroll. Gainsborough

51

Some other films made in the thirties were:-
1933 ORDERS IS ORDERS with Cyril Maude, James Gleason, Charlotte Greenwood, Ray Milland and Cedric Hardwicke. Directed by Walter Forde.
An army barracks is disrupted by an American film company.
Another visitor from Hollywood was London born Boris Karloff who came to Shepherd's Bush to play:-
1933 THE GHOUL with Cedric Harwicke, Ralph Richardson and Kathleen Harrison. Directed by T. Hayes Hunter. Make up by Heinrich Heitfeld.
1933 In May the Prince of Wales visited Gaumont British studios and met Tom Walls on the set of **NEVER COME BACK** which also starred Anne Grey.
1933 SLEEPING CAR with Madeleine Carroll, Ivor Novello and Stanley Holloway. Directed by Anatole Litvac.
A girl on the run goes through a marriage ceremony with a sleeping car attendant thinking it a pretence but finds it is for real. It was an adaption from a stage play.
1934 WALTZ TIME was adapted from Strauss's operetta 'Die Fledermaus' by A.P. Herbert and directed by Williame Thiele. Evelyn Laye played Rosalinde, Gino Malo Adele and Fritz Schultz, Eisenstein.
1934 THE IRON DUKE with Gladys Cooper and George Arliss who played one of his many character roles, The Duke Of Wellington. It was directed by Victor Saville.

The Prince of Wales visit to the studios, 1933. Picture Show

Evelyn Laye and Gino Malo in Waltz Time. Gainsborough

Evelyn Laye. Gainsborough.

Fritz Schulz. Waltz Time 1933. Gainsborough.

53

1934 GAUMONT BRITISH NEWSREELS 1915-1959

The Newsreels with their famous town crier introduction formed an important part of cinema programmes. In the thirties the camera teams were sent out in a Rolls-Royce under the direction of the immensley dapper and flamboyant Castleton Knight. The processing was done at Lime Grove and David Lean as a youth, in his first job, worked there. He went on to make great films including Brief Encounter and A Passage to India.

Gaumont British Newsreel unit on location.

A cutting room at The Gainsborough Studios. Picture Show

The Man They Couldn't Arrest 1933. Gainsborough

The Night of The Party 1934. Michael Powell directing Leslie Banks in the dock. Gainsborough

55

1934 THE MAN THEY COULDN'T ARREST with Renee Clare, Hugh Wakefield and Gordon Harker. Directed by T. Hayes Hunter.

1934 Michael Powell directed four films for Michael Balcon in his years engagement:-

THE NIGHT OF THE PARTY with Jane Baxter where a game of murder at a party leads to a real one.

THE FIRE RAISERS with Leslie Banks and Anne Grey which was suggested by a true story of a city insurance assesor of repute who was arrested and convicted of arson.

THE RED ENSIGN with Leslie Banks playing a Glasgow shipbuilder. This film like the previous one had a budget of £12,000.

THE PHANTOM LIGHT with Binnie Hale and Gordon Harker who played the keeper of a reputedly haunted Welsh lighthouse.

Michael Powell wasn't very proud of his efforts for Gaumont British but went on to make some great pictures like The Red Shoes, A Matter of Life and Death and Black Narcissus.

1934 LITTLE FRIEND directed by Berthold Viertel gave Nova Pilbeam her first film part at fourteen. A very young Jimmy Hanley also starred in this Margaret Kennedy story of a child's experience of family breakup.

1935 ME AND MARLBOROUGH with Cicely Courtneidge, Tom Walls, Cecil Parker and Alfred Drayton. Directed by Victor Saville.

A soldier is accused of spying and his wife takes her place in Marlborough's army, suitably disguised to clear his name.

Little Friend 1934. Nova Pilbeam in her first film, aged 14. Gainsborough

Rhodes of Africa 1936. Michael Balcon, Jesse Laskey visiting U.S. producer, Walter Huston and Berthold Viertel.

Rhodes of Africa 1936. Walter Huston in the studio. Gainsborough

57

In **1936**, George Arliss made three films for Gainsborough:-
EAST MEETS WEST with Godfrey Tearle, Lucie Manheim and John Laurie.
HIS LORDSHIP with Rene Ray. Both Directed by Herbert Mason.
DR SYN with Margaret Lockwood and John Loder. Directed by Milton Rosmer at Islington, it was his last film.
1936 THE GREAT BARRIER with Richard Arlen, Antoinette Collier and Lilli Palmer directed by Milton Rosmer. This film concerned the building of the Canadian Pacific Railway and reviews speak of *scenes of grandeur.* Whether they built the Canadian Rockies in the studio at Lime Grove is questionable although a Swiss Alp and Venice were built there at other times.
1934 Robert Flaherty's MAN OF ARAN was a Gainsborough film shot on location.
Great things were created in the studios at Lime Grove but often the expansive backgrounds needed were too taxing for the art direction and location shooting was done.
1936 RHODES OF AFRICA with Walter Huston as Cecil Rhodes and Oscar Holmolka as Kruger, Basil Sydney, Lewis Casson, Peggy Ashcroft and Bernard Lee. Directed by Berthold Viertel.
Some of this Gaumont British film was also shot on location. It tells the story of Cecil Rhodes, the rough-hewn diamond miner who became Prime Minister of Cape Colony.
Solid, worthy, humourless, it unrolls its eleven well bred reels with all the technical advantages of 1936. Graham Greene, film critic of The Spectator.
1936 Michael Balcon joined Anglo American films, the British wing of Metro Goldwyn Mayer to co-produce good quality films but left after the first film A Yank at Oxford as he couldn't get on with Louis B. Mayer. He left to become an independent producer at Ealing. Edward Black became Head of Studio Production in his place. It was said of him as a producer that *he would always listen to an actor's opinion.*

1937 Gaumont British had 345 cinemas on their circuit at this time.
1937-9 Gaumont British was deep in financial crisis and Lime Grove closed from January 1937-1939. However Margaret Lockwood made The Lady Vanishes with Alfred Hitchcock, Bank Holiday 1937, A Girl Must Live 1939 and The Girl in the News 1940 with Carol Reed at the Islington Studios.

Rhodes of Africa 1936. Africa at Shepherd's Bush. Basil Sydney, Walter Huston and Ndaniso Kumalo. Gainsborough

Night Train To Munich 1939. Rex Harrison, Margaret Lockwood and Paul Henreid. Gainsborough

Night Train to Munich 1939. Basil Radford and Naunton Wayne. Gainsborough

1939 On the outbreak of the Second World War all cinemas were closed as the government thought that during bombing they would be a danger to the public. A very astute man J. Arthur Rank bought up the empty cinemas, many of which had belonged to the Ostrer Brothers. The government soon reversed their policy when bombing didn't immediately begin. Edward Black and Michael Balcon persuaded the Board of Trade of the value of the film industry in Wartime and they realised that it was good for public morale, in providing entertainment and propaganda.

Gaumont British had always produced newsreels, which were valuable in supplying the news people were anxious to see.

1939 J. Arthur Rank now had influence over Gainsborough Pictures and became Chairman of Gaumont British in succession to Isadore Ostrer who retired to Arizona.

1942 Lime Grove Studios belonged to the Rank organisation. The Ostrers still had some influence and Maurice Ostrer appeared on film credits as in Charge of Production but in reality it was Edward Black who was responsible for some of Lime Grove's biggest successes.

1939 The Islington Studios were closed at the outbreak of War. Being beneath the power station chimney, which supplied current to the Metropolitan Railway it was considered too dangerous a situation in the event of air raids. Production moved to Shepherd's Bush.

British Film production was put at the disposal of the Ministry of Information who encouraged escapist and propaganda flavoured productions. A film already begun at Islington was completed at Lime Grove, much being shot on the roof. It was:-

The Gainsborough Studios, Islington. Picture Show

Band Wagon 1939 Arthur Askey, Richard Murdoch and Pat Kirkwood. Gainsborough

Kipps 1940. The cameramen wear tin hats. Gainsborough

61

1939 BAND WAGON with Arthur Askey, Richard Murdoch and Pat Kirkwood. Jack Hylton and his band were featured and it was directed by Marcel Varnel. It was a film version of a familiar radio comedy, just the thing to cheer a wartime public.
Another spy comedy in production was:-
1939 NIGHT TRAIN TO MUNICH with Margaret Lockwood and Rex Harrison. Scripts by Frank Launder and Sidney Gilliat and directed by Carol Reed. This film was obviously inspired by the success of The Lady Vanishes and was about a British agent posing as a Nazi in order to rescue a Czech inventor. In the cast was Austrian Paul von Henreid, in transit before going to Hollywood and his success in Casablanca. Basil Radford and Naunton Wayne provided much of the comedy again and represented the Englishmen who were likely to defeat Adolf Hitler with their stiff upper lips alone. During the filming a large mirror fell just missing Margaret Lockwod and Rex Harrison and 'flu went through the cast and crew but Carol Reed produced it on schedule, in June 1939 as he had a reputation for doing. Margaret Lockwood had caught chickenpox during the shooting of The Girl in the News but Carol Reed still brought the film in on time. Rex Harrison and Carol Reed both lived in Chelsea at this time and joined the Chelsea Home Guard.
1939 CHARLEY'S BIG HEARTED AUNT with Arthur Askey and Phyllis Calvert. Directed by Walter Forde. A not very good version of the famous farce with the popular comedian in the title role. Moore Marriott and Graham Moffatt were in the cast.

Kipps 1940. A tin hat on the lighting platform. Gainsborough

Kipps 1940. Michael Redgrave, Edward Rigby and Hermione Baddeley. Gainsborough

Kipps 1940. Michael Wilding, Michael Redgrave, Max Adrian and Diana Wynyard in a Beaton interior. Gainsborough

1940 In July the studio was loaned to Twentieth Century Fox and Carol Reed directed a large production based on an H.G. Wells novel:-

KIPPS with Michael Redgrave, Phyllis Calvert, Diana Wynyard, Michael Wilding and Arthur Riscoe. H.G. Wells approved the screenplay by Sidney Gilliat. It was designed by Vetchinsky who had done many previous productions at Lime Grove. Costumes were by Cecil Beaton, also some interiors which were lavish reconstructions of the Edwardian style. The story's message was the hatefulness of class snobbery. Carol Reed thought this was worth delivering to a wartime audience. He thought they wanted to be reminded of the nostalgia of an age so recently past and quite different from the austerity of wartime England. He also thought they were ready for the serious stuff and would be bored by the series of comedies which were being served up to them.

Carol Reed and Michael Redgrave lived in the same block of flats in Grosvenor Gardens in Belgravia and travelled to Lime Grove by car together at 6.00 am, to start shooting at 8.00 am. Michael Redgrave took sleeping pills in order to get a good nights sleep through 'the Blitz' which had started. He was playing a young Kipps and needed his 'beauty sleep'. In the evenings Reed and Redgrave talked and when Redgrave retired, Reed met Diana Wynyard with whom he had a secret liaison, they married in 1942.

Carol Reed always stopped the car at Lime Grove gates each morning and called to the gatekeeper, *'Hey George, what do you think of the film so far?'* George was usually positive but when a game of anagrams in one scene gave him trouble, Carol Reed re-shot the scene although the cast thought it rather good. Reed was so anxious to give the film mass appeal.

Reed and Redgrave thought they might be 'called up' at any time and Michael Wilding only got his part because, John Mills the first choice, had been called up. Work on KIPPS in September 1940 was often delayed by air raids and Reed was a stickler for schedules. Michael Wilding told how parties of roof spotters were organised to give the alarm if bombers were spotted directly overhead, thus reducing the time lost on daily shooting schedules. Many of the crew now slept in the basement of Lime Grove to avoid travelling through the heavier raids on Central and East London. Phyllis Calvet 'bombed out' from her mother's home, converted a studio waiting room into a bed-sit and lived there whilst the film was

Kipps 1940. Diana Wynyard. Gainsborough

64

Kipps 1940. The Crystal Palace at Shepherd's Bush. Michael Redgrave, Phyllis Calvert. Gainsborough

Kipps 1940. Michael Wilding. Gainsborough

Kipps 1940. Michael Redgrave. Gainsborough

65

being made. The technicians worked wearing tin hats looking very much like gun crew.

1940 Carol Reed finished the film on time and the premiere was on the 21st May at Folkestone, the film's setting. It was only 25 miles from Occupied France and it was his way of showing 'we could carry on'. Seeing this cool Edwardian drama today there is no sign at all of the difficulties in making it or in any of the other films being made at the time:-

1940 GASBAGS was a fast moving knock-a-bout with the Crazy Gang. Directed by Marcel Varnel. The six popular comedians who as airmen were conveyed to Germany on a barrage balloon to cause havoc there!

1940 NEUTRAL PORT with Will Fyffe and Phyllis Calvert. Directed by Maurice Elvey. A merchant navy captain sabotages a U Boat.

1940 FOR FREEDOM with Will Fyffe. Directed by Maurice Elvey.
The story of the Battle of the River Plate and the sinking of the Graf Spee (1939). It used actual newsreel material. Will Fyffe was originally a music hall artist but these were two straight parts he played. Another had been 'Owd Bob' at Islington in 1938.

1941 I THANK YOU with Arthur Askey and Richard Murdoch. Directed by Marcel Varnel. Another comedy by this popular radio team together with Moore Mariott, Graham Moffatt and Kathleen Harrison. Three character actors who appeared in so many Gainsborough films.

1941 THE GHOST TRAIN with Arthur Askey and Richard Murdoch and Kathleen Harrison. Directed by Walter Forde.
A remake of the film made by Gainsborough in 1931. This very successful play was written by Arthur Ridley who found fame later in life as Private Godfrey in TV's 'Dad's Army'. He first went on the stage in 1914, served in the First World War, was invalided out, continued on the stage and was in the last episode of Dad's Army in 1977. Gainsborough also filmed another of his plays Easy Money in 1948 at Pinewood.

1941 HI GANG! with Bebe Daniels, Ben Lyon and Vic Oliver. Directed by Marcel Varnel. A popular radio show translated into a film.

Will Fyffe. Gainsborough

The Young Mr Pitt 1941. Phyllis Calvert and Robert Donat. Gainsborough

The Young Mr Pitt 1941. Street scene. Gainsborough

Cottage to Let 1941. George Cole, Muriel Aked and Jeanne de Casalis. Gainsborough

1941 COTTAGE TO LET with Alistair Sim, John Mills, Michael Wilding and George Cole. Directed by Anthony Asquith.

A comedy thriller. John Mills quite out of character played a Nazi spy unmasked by a cockney evacuee, George Cole.

John Mills had been discharged from the Army and in his autobiography remembers, cycling to Shepherd's Bush from Knightsbridge through the 'black out' to make this film. This was at the height of the Blitz. He and his wife were 'bombed out' at the completion of the film.

1942 KING ARTHUR WAS A GENTLEMAN with Arthur Askey, Jack Train and Evelyn Dall. Directed by Marcel Varnel at Islington.

A comedy with Arthur in the Army.

1942 BACK ROOM BOY with Arthur Askey, Googie Withers, Moore Marriott and Graham Moffatt. Directed by Herbert Mason.

IT'S THAT MAN AGAIN with Tommy Handley, Jack Train and Greta Gynt which brought in all the familiar characters from this most popular of all wartime radio comedies. Jack Train's German spy 'Funf' was always a great figure of fun, always the butt of the others' jokes and pranks. Such was the mood on the 'home front' at the time that the populace were made to feel Hitler could be vanquished as easily as 'Funf'.

Carol Reed directed another lavish film with a strong propaganda flavour which showed a Britain blockaded and under daily threat from Napoleon in an earlier age. It was produced by Edward Black for Twentieth Century Fox and was:-

The Young Mr Pitt 1941. The House of Commons. Gainsborough

The Young Mr Pitt 1941. Wig care. Gainsborough

1941 THE YOUNG MR PITT with Robert Donat, John Mills, Robert Morley and Phyllis Calvert. The screenplay was by Frank Launder and Sydney Gilliat. The lavish film sets were by Vetchinsky and Cecil Beaton who also designed the costumes. The building of the sets at Lime Grove and the costumes took months to prepare. The House of Commons and whole eighteenth century streets were built. Robert Donat was under contract to MGM but refused to leave Britain in wartime hence this film was made under contract to Twentieth Century Fox. There were 128 speaking parts. Three months were allocated for the shooting of the film which began at the end of July 1941. The budget was £250,000. It did in fact take six months to make against the background of the bombing of London. Pitt's authentic speeches were an obvious homage to Winston Churchill and a plea to the US to come into the War. Robert Donat had broadcast radio appeals to America. However, Pearl Harbor occurred before the end of the filming in 1942.

Carol Reed joined up at the end of the film and formed The Army Film Unit consisting of himself as Director, Thorold Dickenson as Producer and Eric Ambler and Peter Ustinov as Scriptwriters! They were to make instructional films for the Army on commando raids but this was cancelled after the disastrous Dieppe raid. The morale boosting films they did were THE WAY AHEAD 1943 and THE TRUE GLORY 1944.

At Lime Grove they were making:-

1942 UNCENSORED with Eric Portman, Phyllis Calvert and Griffith Jones. Directed by Anthony Asquith.
A melodrama set in Nazi occupied Brussels.

1943 MILLIONS LIKE US with Eric Portman, Patricia Roc, Gordon Jackson, Anne Crawford, Basil Radford, Naunton Wayne and Moore Marriott.
Launder and Gilliat directed and wrote the script.
The story told of the home front during the War.

1943 MISS LONDON LTD with Arthur Askey, Jack Train, Evelyn Dall, Jean Kent and Anne Shelton. Directed by Val Guest.
'A flagwaving light entertainment with popular performers of the time'.

1943 BEES IN PARADISE with Arthur Askey and Jean Kent. Directed by Val Guest.
The story was about four airmen marooned on a desert island ruled by women. It was so disastrous that Arthur Askey didn't make another film for ten years.

1943 DEAR OCTOPUS with Margaret Lockwood, Michael Wilding and Celia Johnson. Directed by Harold French. There was a large cast list of Britain's finest character actors, including Graham Moffatt again. The story concerned members of a well-to-do British family reuniting for Golden Wedding celebrations. It was taken from a Dodie Smith play, and typical of the thirties. It was well done and entertaining and must have been refreshing after those endless comic spy stories.

1943 WE DIVE AT DAWN with John Mills and Eric Portman. Directed by Anthony Asquith.
A good yarn about a British submarine disabled in the Baltic in wartime. John Mills in the Navy again, perhaps they used the large water tank beneath Stage 4(F) at Lime Grove studios where so many naval battles were fought, including the Battle of Trafalgar in The Young Mr Pitt!

The Man in Grey 1943. Margaret Lockwood and James Mason. Gainsborough

1943 Gainsborough at this time was making 18-20 films a year and you can deduce from the above titles that some were memorable, others now forgotten but they served their purpose in entertaining their audiences at the height of the War. Now we are about to enter the Gainsborough 'Gothic' period, a series of escapist romances which if you saw them in your teens as I did, you will never have forgotten. Harry Ostrer is reported as the discoverer of Lady Eleanor Smith's novel, The Man in Grey which started the run of very successful costume romances for Gainsborough. All appropriately introduced by the Gainsborough lady who dipped her Ostrich plumed hat to the audience at the start of each film. The stories were taken from popular novels and proved a great draw with cinema audiences which reached 30,000,000 in 1946. Very often the plots starred James Mason and Margaret Lockwood as the very attractive villains and Phyllis Calvert and Stewart Granger as the ill starred heroine and hero. The plots gave a new freedom of expression for actresses in particular. Jean Kent, Patricia Roc and others joined the cast lists. James Mason, now married to Pamela, daughter of Isadore Ostrer, signed with Gainsborough for THE MAN IN GREY and a further five films, but only four were made.

1943 THE MAN IN GREY with James Mason, Phyllis Calvert, Margaret Lockwood and Stewart Granger.

James Mason didn't get on with the director, Leslie Arliss and he, *attributes his ability to play the monstrously nasty Lord Rohan to sheer bad temper* and *claims none of the credit for the character colour.* The story went, in Regency times, Lord Rohan marries the sweet trusting Melissa, who invites her scheming schoolfriend to join the household as her companion. The schoolfriend, instead becomes Lord Rohan's companion and tries to supplant Lady Rohan. She arranges for a librarian to be employed whom she knows is already in love with Melissa

The Man in Grey 1943. James Mason as Lord Rohan. Gainsborough

The Wicked Lady 1944. James Mason at the Gibbet, a studio shot. Gainsborough

The Wicked Lady 1944. Technicians and cast at Lime Grove. Gainsborough

73

and the expected result occurs. There is a fine 'horse-whipping' scene when Rohan discovers his mistress's treachery.

The Man in Grey was a flop at the London premiere but the film was a success in the provinces and there was a second London premiere.

1944 FANNY BY GASLIGHT with Phylis Calvert, James Mason, Stewart Granger, Jean Kent and Margaretta Scott. Directed by Anthony Asquith.

A Victorian melodrama from a novel by Michael Sadlier where the illegitimate daughter of a cabinet minister is saved from the lustful lord, James Mason.

Edward Black left Gaumont British in 1944 to be replaced by Sydney Box as Head of Production.

1945 THE WICKED LADY with Margaret Lockwood, James Mason, Patricia Roc, Griffith Jones and Michael Rennie. Directed by Leslie Arliss.

In the days of Charles II the wicked Lady Skelton, Margaret Lockwood, bored with the rich husband she has stolen from her best friend, Patricia Roc, when invited to the wedding takes to the road as a highwaywoman. There she meets highwayman James Mason. She finds the excitement she craved and after murders and a hanging she dies a colourful death despised by the man she loves, Michael Rennie.

Margaret Lockwood recalls memories of THE WICKED LADY almost 40 years after it appeared, to Phillip Jenkinson in the 'Radio Times'.

The film was based on a best seller which in turn was based on a true story, 'The Life and Death of the Wicked Lady Skelton' by Magdalen King-Hall.

'I think that's what initially drew me to the part – that it wasn't all some silly schoolgirl romance, but that it was also based on fact. Of course I'm sure a lot of embroidering happened along the way'. Asked where the exteriors had been shot, she said, *'90% of the movie was shot at Lime Grove studios although some exteriors were done at Burnham Beeches.'*

What about those very wobbly back-projection scenes where she and Griffith Jones were supposed to be going for a trot?

'Oh, that was ALL studio, and of course the wretched horses would not keep in time with the back projection. Leslie Arliss, the director, insisted we used real horses and not "rockers", but not only had we to keep the horses in time, we had to stop them wandering left or right. I think that's why the mid-shots and close-ups look so strange. At times we were almost at right-angles with the back-projection screen.'

Asked what James Mason thought of the film, she said,

Well, it's funny you should ask, because we met up a week or so ago, and he was waxing quite nostalgic about it. Of course he was marvelous in the film but I had to remind him that after almost every shot he'd stalk off the set muttering, 'ruddy codswallop!'

All the reviews of the film Margaret Lockwood recalled were scathing in their condemnation of its bawdiness.

I was amazed to read the press and see words like 'salacious' and 'immoral', especially as Queen Mary had said to me at the reception after the Royal Film Performance how much she had enjoyed it. The newspapers even claim that part of the soundtrack had been edited at the Royal screening, but that was pure nonsense. Strangely enough, it was the American distributors and the Hays Code that caused the bother. They thought my cleavage was too low, so for the American version we had to re-shoot certain close-ups with added lace across my bosom.

Michael Rennie. Gainsborough

Jean Kent. Gainsborough

Patricia Roc. Gainsborough

Anne Crawford. Gainsborough

The Wicked Lady 1944. A studio shot. Gainsborough

Asked whether playing such a wicked lady had brought adverse publicity or nasty letters she said,
Not one I think everyone was so relieved after the War to see such a smashing bit of pure escapism, the wickedness of it all quite escaped them. No, on the contrary, they wanted more. Leslie, the director, said to me, "well Margaret, should we do a 'Return of the Wicked Lady'? But I respectfully declined, apart from the fact she came to a sticky end, it was the kind of thing you could only do as a one-off. I think that's one of the reasons its still remembered so vividly nearly 40 years after".

The Wicked Lady 1944. Margaret Lockwood. Ted Reed

Victory Wedding 1944. Jessie Matthews directing John Mills and Dulcie Gray. Gainsborough

Madonna Of The Seven Moons 1944. Stewart Granger and Phyllis Calvert. Gainsborough

These were the three great melodramas and there were others to follow but in complete contrast, I must return to 1944 when Jessie Matthews visited Lime Grove one day. Maurice Ostrer saw how much she grasped of the technical side of film making and persuaded her to direct a film, it was:-

1944 VICTORY WEDDING with John Mills and Dulcie Gray. It was only a 20 min short being made for the National Savings Committee's, 'Salute the Soldier' campaign but 'The Star' commented, *It is directed with a pleasant vein of sentiment and with so many neat little touches that it is evident Miss Matthews has learned much about the technical side of filming from her experiences at Shepherd's' Bush.*

1944 A PLACE OF ONE'S OWN with James Mason, Barbara Mullen and Margaret Lockwood. Directed by Bernard Knowles. From a novel by Osbert Sitwell. Designed by Rex Whistler. This was an Edwardian ghost story where James Mason played an elderly caring husband. C.A. Lejeune, the critic called it, *A fine piece of work... gripping, marvellous, outstanding, eerie, perky, beautiful, lovely and different.* But for most of James Mason's fans it was too different and they were pleased when he returned to the sadist again. He said *they want a lady killer or better still a lady basher.*

1945 THEY WERE SISTERS with Phyllis Calvert, Dulcie Gray, Anne Crawford and Pamela Kellino (who played his daughter) was made at Islington. Directed by Arthur Crabtree from a novel by Dorothy Whipple where a sadistic husband persecutes his timid wife, Dulcie Gray. Dulcie Gray was visited on the set by her husband Michael Dennison who was just about to leave the Army. A director, Harold French, remembered him from that visit and cast them together later when he was making My Brother Jonathan 1947 and Michael Dennison alone at Lime Grove in The Blind Goddess in 1947.

James Mason had completed only five films and his contract with Gainsborough ran out. In 1946 he made Odd Man Out with Carol Reed for Two Cities and realised some of his potential but in 1947 after 40 films and completely dissatisfied with what he considered, *the mismanagement of the English cinema in the person of J. Arthur Rank,* he left for Hollywood. Meanwhile the Gainsborough romances continued.

1944 MADONNA OF THE SEVEN MOONS with Phyllis Calvert, Stewart Granger, Patricia Roc, Jean Kent and John Stuart. Directed by Arthur Crabtree. A respectable wife has a second life as a gipsy and exchanges her husband, John Stuart, for a dashing gipsy, Stewart Granger. Labelled *novelettish balderdash* it was a great box office success!

1944 2000 WOMEN with Phyllis Calvert, Jean Kent, Patricia Roc, Dulcie Gray, Flora Robson and Thora Hird. A story of women in a French concentration camp. Described as, *totally implausible.*

Madonna Of The Seven Moons 1944. Phyllis Calvert. Gainsborough

78

Daybreak 1946. Eric Portman, Ann Todd, cast and technicians. Gainsborough

Waterloo Road 1944. Pint sized John Mills knocks out Stewart Granger! Gainsborough

1944 LOVE STORY with Margaret Lockwood, Stewart Granger, Patricia Roc, and Tom Walls. Directed by Leslie Arliss.
In a Cornish setting a half-blind airman falls in love with a pianist with a weak heart. *A tear jerker with a good musical background.* Herbert Bath's Cornish Rhapsody played by Eileen Joyce.

1944 GIVE US THE MOON with Margaret Lockwood, Vic Oliver, Peter Graves and Jean Simmons. A whimsical comedy set in a post-War London club. Not a success.

1944 WATERLOO ROAD with John Mills, Stewart Granger, Jean Kent and Joy Shelton. Directed by Sidney Gilliat. A Wartime love story, a soldier goes A.W.O.L. when he hears his wife has taken up with a petty crook. A very atmospheric and successful film.

1945 Miss Esme Jempson dealt with fan mail at this time and handled 2,000 letters a week. Before the War 8,000 was normal. Stewart Granger, Phyllis Calvert and Margaret Lockwood got 300-500 letters a week. Close runners-up were John Mills, Patricia Roc and Jean Kent.

A soldier in the Middle East asked Pat Roc *to write to his wife and tell her how much he loved her as she would express it so much better than he.* An admirer from South Africa sent Jean Kent a coconut, unobtainable in England in Wartime. 'The Star'. 9.2.45.

Lime Grove had A BRIDAL HIRE SERVICE FOR SERVICE BRIDES.

You could hire *the cobweb lace dress worn by Margaret Lockwood in Love Story and which had originally cost £110.* The cost for hire was £2.2.0 for six days. *Dulcie Gray's cream satin dress worn in They Were Sisters which originally cost £60* and Phyllis Calvert's and Anne Crawford's bridesmaids dresses from the same film which had originally cost £70 were also available. *Joy Shelton's satin wedding dress from Waterloo Road* only cost a modest £21 originally, however still an expensive dress in those days.

They Were Sisters 1945. Phyllis Calvert, Dulcie Gray and James Mason. Shot at Islington. Gainsborough

1945 I'LL BE YOUR SWEETHEART with Margaret Lockwood, Michael Rennie and Vic Oliver. Directed by Val Guest.

A musical romance set in 1900. Michael Rennie was invalided out of the forces a few months before he appeared in The Wicked Lady and this film.

1945 THE RAKE'S PROGRESS with Rex Harrison, Lilli Palmer, Jean Kent and Guy Middleton. Directed by Sidney Gilliat. Screenplay by Frank Launder and Sidney Gilliat. The titles were drawn by Topolski.

The story of a thirties playboy, a debonair cad who redeems himself in War service.

When, as a student Rex Harrison crowns the Martyr's memorial Oxford with a chamber pot a top hat had to be substituted for the American version.

1946 CARAVAN with Stewart Granger, Jean Kent, Anne Crawford and Robert Helpman. Directed by Arthur Crabtree.

Stewart Granger's character is nursed back to life from near death by a gipsy girl, Jean Kent, who falls in love with him.

The Rakes Progress 1945. Rex Harrison and Lilli Palmer. Gainsborough

1946 THE MAGIC BOW with Stewart Granger, Jean Kent, Phyllis Calvert and Dennis Price. Directed by Bernard Knowles.

The early life of Paganini, the violin virtuoso. 'Yehudi Menuhin recorded the sound track, the first he had ever done. It was recorded at the HMV studios with the London Symphony Orchestra and Basil Cameron. He used the actual Stradivarius which had belonged to Paganini'. Reported 'The Evening Standard'. 11.5.45.

James Mason was offered the part and practised the violin for some time in his dressing room whilst touring with his wife Pamela in Gaslight. When he saw the script concerned mainly the love life, rather than the musical career of Paganini, he turned the part down. As a gesture of goodwill he sent the bow he had bought to Stewart Granger.

1946 THE ROOT OF ALL EVIL with Phyllis Calvert, Michael Rennie and John McCallum. A jilted woman gets even with her ex-boyfriend.

1946 DAYBREAK with Eric Portman, Ann Todd and Maxwell Reed. Directed by Compton Bennett. A gloomy dockside melodrama delayed for two years after shooting by censorship cuts and finally released in 1948.

1947 DEAR MURDERER with Eric Portman, Greta Gynt, Dennis Price and Jack Warner. Directed by Arthur Crabtree. An adulterous triangle taken from a popular play. Jack Warner made his first appearance as a policeman in this film.

1947 THE BLIND GODDESS with Eric Portman, Anne Crawford, Michael Dennison and Hugh Williams. Directed by Harold French. A courtroom drama from a Patrick Hasting's play.

1947 WHEN THE BOUGH BREAKS with Patricia Roc, Rosamund John, Bill Owen and Patrick Holt. Directed by Lawrence Huntington. A baby is adopted and later the mother regrets it. This was a controversial social document significant to the time.

1947 HOLIDAY CAMP with Jack Warner, Kathleen Harrison, Flora Robson, Dennis Price and Jimmy Hanley. Directed by Ken Annakin. From a story by Godfrey Winn. A murderer on the prowl amongst the campers. Ted Willis, author of Dixon of Dock Green was one of the screen writers. Jack Warner and Kathleen Harrison appeared together in one sequence for the first time as The Huggetts, later included in three films at Islington before appearing in the nine year radio series. Jack Warner told how they had *one scene in this film sitting on a cliff top in brilliant sunshine. He was dressed in a cricket shirt, Kathleen Harrison in a light summer frock. It was in fact filmed in the studio at Lime Grove with snow on the ground outside and it was freezing inside as well.* Jack also tells how Jimmy Hanley's son and Jack's godson had a part in the film as a baby girl. That baby has grown up to be Jeremy Hanley, Minister of State.

Holiday Camp 1947. Jack Warner and godson Jeremy Hanley. Gainsborough

It's Not Cricket 1948. Naunton Wayne and Basil Radford as "Charters and Caldicott". Gainsborough

It's Not Cricket 1948. Basil Radford, Diana Dors and Naunton Wayne. Gainsborough

1948 IT'S NOT CRICKET with Basil Radford, Naunton Wayne and Maurice Denham. Directed by Alfred Roome.

Charters and Caldicott, the cricket enthusiasts from The Lady Vanishes catching Nazi spies. This one seems left over from Wartime productions.

1948 BROKEN JOURNEY with Phyllis Calvert and James Donald. Directed by Ken Annakin. A plane crash in the Swiss Alps, built at Lime Grove, the story of the survivors. Ken Annakin was very experienced at location shooting and some filming was done in Switzerland.

1948 QUARTET with Dirk Bogarde, George Cole, Linden Travers, Basil Radford and Naunton Wayne.

Four stories introduced by the author, Somerset Maugham and directed by four different directors, The Facts of Life by Ralph Smart, The Alien Corn by Harold French, The Kite by Arthur Crabtree and The Colonel's Lady by Ken Annakin. This was Dirk Bogarde's second film appearance. One of the messengers at Lime Grove, taking visitors around used to pause and say, *this is Jessie Matthews studio you know? We always make a bob and say "God Bless you Jessie"*. Dirk Bogarde was intrigued with this and visited Jessie Matthews at her home 'Evergreen' in Farnham, Surrey, and was captivated with her. He became a fan. Trio and Encore other films in this group were made elsewhere. The Islington studios were back in production by this time now that the War was ended and sometimes its difficult to discover where the different productions were made.

The Alien Corn, Quartet 1948. Dirk Bogarde, Raymond Lovell and Françoise Rosay. Gainsborough

The Bad Lord Byron 1948. Sketch for the ballroom, Melbourne House. Gainsborough

The Bad Lord Byron 1948. The set for the ballroom, Melbourne House. Gainsborough

1948 A BOY A GIRL AND A BIKE with John McCallum and Honor Blackman. Directed by Ralph Smart.
A comedy drama by Ted Willis about a Yorkshire cycling club.

1948 THE CALENDAR with John McCallum and Greta Gynt. Directed by Arthur Crabtree.
A racecourse melodrama previously made at Lime Grove in 1931.

1948 PORTRAIT FROM LIFE with Mai Zetterling and Robert Beatty. Directed by Terence Fisher.
Melodrama about an amnesia victim.

1948 MY BROTHER'S KEEPER with George Cole, David Tomlinson and Jack Warner. Directed by Alfred Roome.
A social melodrama. Two convicts on the run, handcuffed together.

1948 THE BAD LORD BYRON with Dennis Price, Mai Zetterling, Joan Greenwood and Linden Travers. Directed by David MacDonald.
This was the last of the large stylish Gainsborough costume films at Lime Grove which began with The Man in Grey. It told the story of Lord Byron and his loves. Venice was re-built at Shepherd's Bush to match the location shots actually done in Venice.

The Bad Lord Byron 1948. Dennis Price. Gainsborough

The Bad Lord Byron 1948. Dennis Price and Joan Greenwood. Gainsborough

Christopher Columbus 1948. Banquet scene. Gainsborough

87

1948 THE ASTONISHED HEART with Noel Coward, Margaret Leighton and Celia Johnson. Directed by Terence Fisher, from a play by Noel Coward.
A psychiatrist falls in love with two women and kills himself.
Michael Redgrave left the leading part, after shooting began.
1948 CHRISTOPHER COLUMBUS with Fredric March, Florence Eldridge, Francis L. Sullivan, Linden Travers, Katherine Ryan and Derek Bond. Directed by David MacDonald.
This was the only colour film made at Lime Grove. It was a very large production and labelled as a 'prestige' film from the start. The battery of powerful arc lamps made the sets very hot and uncomfortable. There were experts on the historical accuracy of details. The wardrobe master was W. Neale. The hairdresser and wig-maker Elsie Alder. The music was by Sir Arthur Bliss. The extras were paid £2.00 per day. 'The Evening Reporter' said, *The sets were so elaborate and beautiful it seems a pity it will be destroyed in a few days.* Florence Eldridge, Mrs Fredric March, played Queen Isabella of Spain. It was completed on 12.10.48 and when shown the world pronounced it, *a tediously paced historical account of undramatic events.* Having seen it recently, I can confirm the sets and colour were good and the production more creditable than the contemporary critic indicates. Perhaps the historical events are to be blamed. If Columbus had discovered Manhattan Island instead of Cuba it would have made a better story.

Christopher Columbus 1948. Sydney Box and Fredric March. Gainsborough

Travellers Joy 1949. Colin Gordon, John McCallum, Googie Withers and technicians. Gainsborough

Travellers Joy 1949. Googie Withers and Geoffry Sumner. Gainsborough

89

1948 HELTER SKELTER with David Tomlinson, Carol Marsh, Jimmy Edwards, Richard Hearne, Jon Pertwee and Terry Thomas. Directed by Ralph Thomas.
This was a scatty comedy supposedly about an heiress with hiccups being helped by the staff of the BBC! It tried everything and the script was improvised as they went along. Anyone who could come up with a funny line, stars or technicians, found it included. Costumes were even borrowed from Christopher Columbus which was filming at the same time. A baby elephant was brought onto the set. Richard Hearne played a dozen parts, including 'The Gainsborough Girl'. Jon Pertwee filmed the last scene on Stage 5 before the closing of the studio.
1949 DON'T EVERY LEAVE ME with Jimmy Hanley, Petula Clark, Anthony Newley and Edward Rigby. Directed by Arthur Crabtree.
An ex-convict and grandfather abducts two teenagers.
The BBC and James Mason speak of this *as the last film made at Lime Grove* but that seems to be just artistic licence as according to a contemporary newscutting, the last was:-
1949 TRAVELLERS JOY with Googie Withers and John McCallum. Directed by Ralph Thomas.
A divorced couple are stranded in Sweden by lack of funds. The story was from a popular play by Arthur MacRae.

Don't Ever Leave Me 1949. Jimmy Hanley and Petula Clark. Gainsborough

Googie Withers. Gainsborough

The newspaper reporter who visited the studio said, *Googie Withers was the last star to be filmed on Stage 4, the largest of them all, before the cameras were shut down.* He also reported that *Pamela Hitchin was posing as 'The Gainsborough Lady' at the same time on another stage.*

The next Gainsborough costume drama So Long at the Fair with Jean Simmons and Dirk Bogarde was shot at Pinewood. Produced by Sydney Box and directed by Terence Fisher and Anthony Darnborough.

In 1945 Sydney Box became Managing Director of Gainsborough Pictures. James Mason said of him, *when he visited the set each day his beaming presence gave the impression that for him each new day was a new adventure.*

This was high praise indeed from someone who disliked most producers and directors. When Lime Grove closed he went on to produce other Gainsborough films with a lot of his old team of directors. In view of the last I'm not sure how genuine were some of his reported statements. The tears could have been the natural result of sadness at leaving the studios which have always inspired a great deal of attachment in people.

The papers report:-

2.3.1949 *Mr Sidney Box addressed 550 men and women at the Shepherd's Bush studios with tears in his eyes, 'everybody is going, the producers, the directors and writers, all the people at the top as well as technicians.*

3.3.1949 *550 workers decided to organise a mass demonstration in Hyde Park on Saturday week. Islington studios were to be closed who had 300 employees, making 3,000 and more unemployed in the business at this time.*

3.3.1949 *Twenty employees are to be kept on for duties as firemen and for maintenance work. The editing department is to be kept open to work on films already shot until they were completed and the newsreel facilities, which would be moved elsewhere later.*

Meanwhile, Miss Dolly Smith of Kilburn, sixteen years wardrobe mistress; Harry Caughlin at 73, liftman at £5.13.8 a week, from Westwick Gardens, Shepherd's Bush said, '*I don't know if I'll get another job at my age';* and Len Harris, cameraman at £22 a week; were to lose their jobs. Down in the basement, property master, Arthur Rumsey in pictures since 1922 looked at his thousands of props. He once had a staff of fifty on props but now only thirteen. For Albert Milling, stage hand from Ealing, a shut down will break thirty years connection with the studio. He joined it in 1919 when demobbed from the Army and stayed on through the three year shut-down before the last war. Only ten staff stayed on through this pre-War film depression. These were the human stories in the local paper 'The West London Observer'.

THE TIMES of 3.3.1949 told these facts:-
The Rank Organisation had £4,000,000 available from takings which would enable them to make only 25 films a year at £160,000 each.
'The West London Observer' of 4.11.49 continued:-
The Shepherd's Bush studios were at one time producing a film a month. Big films made there recently were Christopher Columbus and The Bad Lord Byron. Lime Grove is one of the four largest studios in the country.
Outside the studios could be seen a long line of sleek cars. Through the swing doors 'big shots' hurried in and out. Though I have been to the studios many times, I never found my way through the mass of corridors unguided. There were long lines of dressing rooms, publicity offices, offices of the executives – and then abruptly you came upon a padded sliding door with a big notice above it saying 'DON'T ENTER WHEN THE RED LIGHT IS SHOWING' and then when the light changed you slid back the door and were on the set.
A Nostalgic Farewell from A.T. Weisman.
Closing means cutting Gainsborough's sixteen pictures planned to six. Betty Box, who was to have produced five pictures at Shepherd's Bush will now make two at Denham, one was, Little Lambs Eat Ivy. Two others directed by Anthony Darnborough will go to Pinewood. 'The Star'.
'The Cinema Exhibitors Association' said, the imposition of the 45% British (films) quota had disastrous results on British production. Films had to stand and fall on their own appeal, too many fell.
Came news of the closing of Lime Grove. The studios were said to be 'neither modern in plan, nor economical for big film production and that Mr Rank's austerity plans will probably be better served at the Rank studios at Pinewood and Denham which were larger and could be expanded. There was a British film crisis and it was hoped the Government would step in and save the British film industry.' Nothing changes.
25.10.1949 The auction of the contents took over a week in late October. The auctioneers dealt with 2,620 lots and the auction took place on Stage 4.

J. Arthur Rank. R. Gordon Wilson.

THE WEST LONDON OBSERVER FRIDAY NOVEMBER 4, 1949

BBC BUY RANK STUDIOS

VAST TV PRODUCTION CENTRE AT LIME GROVE

Bigger and better programmes

BY A.T. WEISMAN

The announcement on Wednesday that the BBC has bought the Rank film studios at Lime Grove, Shepherd's Bush, in order to expand their television service will reinforce the belief held by many people in the film industry that television will, eventually, supersede films as a medium of popular entertainment.

For, whilst film production is dwindling and film studios are compelled to close down or work to very diminished schedules, television is taking great strides forward.

THE SHEPHERD'S BUSH STUDIOS WERE AT ONE TIME PRODUCING A FILM A MONTH, AND Mr SYDNEY BOX HAD ACTUALLY ANNOUNCED A PROGRAMME OF 19 FILMS IN ONE YEAR WHEN THE FILM CRISIS SET IN AND CURTAILED PRODUCTION.

At the moment one can only speculate on the effect the increase in studio facilities will have on future programmes. But one thing is certain: it will mean BETTER programmes and more of them.

At Alexandra Palace, the present transmission – production centre, there are only two studios, both very small, and producers have to work in extremely cramped space.

Ample space

Plays can be rehearsed before TV cameras only once, on the morning of the broadcast, and this has inevitably detracted from the smoothness of productions. There are also great limitations in the construction of scenery.

At Shepherd's Bush, with its many and spacious workshops where vast palaces have been pre-fabricated, there will be ample space, and no serious difficulties should be encountered in building any set that may be needed.

There will have to be very few alterations in the general lay-out of the studios.

The most important work will be the installation on each "shooting floor" – and it is planned to have five – of a producer's turret: this is an all-glass control room overlooking the studio in which the producer sits during transmission, wearing headphones and directing his camera-men (who also have headphones) by means of a microphone before him.

He instructs them when to "track in," when to "pan," at what angle to approach.

Although each camera-man knows in advance roughly what is required of him from the detailed shooting script with which he is supplied, this business of commanding the unit whilst a programme is on the air inevitably makes for a great deal of suspense and tenseness which film-making cannot match.

TV programmes are actually edited whilst in transmission. The producer in his control room can, by the twist of a knob, cut from one camera to the other. Three cameras are usually in use, two lining up on the next scenes whilst the other is transmitting, and vice-versa on a relief basis.

The screens in the control room show the producer the scene that is on the air, and the scene about to go on the air.

More cameras

Now that studio facilities have been increased, it may well be that more television cameras – say four or five – will be installed; this would make for greater complexity, enable larger productions to be put on and also make rapid "cutting" – changes from one scene to another – possible without confusion.

At Alexandra Palace there is very little space for the camera men to manipulate in, and with cables and wires snaking after the cameras, nothing too complicated can be attempted.

But now that a major film studio has been taken over, it would be possible, in theory, to produce television programmes almost on the same scale as motion pictures.

In some quarters it is thought that Shepherd's Bush might become the first television-film studio.

Much speculation

In recent months there has been much speculation on the advantages of installing television equipment in film studios and making films on television technique.

Alfred Hitchcock's T.M.T.

films "Rope" and "Under Capricorn" were attempts at adapting film-making to television methods.

It seems fairly probable that large scale BBC television productions would be recorded on celluloid for future repetition; this would in effect be making films by television methods.

Film producers toying with this idea – it is supposed to slash costs – would then be able to see how it works out in practice.

Both the BBC and the Rank Organisation refuse to add to their joint statement giving the bare outlines of transaction. It is known that Mr Rank is very interested in the possibilities of television-films, television-studios, and television-cinemas.

Extra significance?

Talks have been going on for the past few months between television and film chiefs. It is not impossible that the taking over by the BBC of Shepherd's Bush Studios has some extra significance such as I have suggested, for only three months ago the BBC refused to buy the same studios.

No official figures are available as to the price paid for the studios. Rumours vary. Some put it as high as £250,000, others at about £100,000.*

Neither figure is spectacular for such immense studios. Many of the films which have been made there have cost more than £250,000, and very few minor productions cost less than £100,000.

To rent studio space costs something like £5,000 a week these days.

The news of the BBC-Rank deal came on the last day of the auction of contents.

With the radio city which is planned at the White City, the television studios at Lime Grove, Hammersmith will be the greatest broadcasting centre in Europe.

*The official figure given was £230,000.

93

1936 Public television transmissions started in England on 26.8.1936, only to be shut down by the Second World War.

1946 It was revived on 7.6.1946 at Alexandra Palace which had only two studios, A and B.

1949 To extend the service Lime Grove was purchased from Gaumont British by the BBC as television studios. It was thought of as a temporary measure until their new television centre was built in Wood Lane, where they had purchased a site in the same year. However, Lime Grove studios were in use by the BBC until 1991, over forty years.

1949 The Postmaster General announced the standardisation of the 405-line transmission. Technical improvements in cameras and equipment advanced considerably and there were about 90,000 TV licences at this time.

Even so there were many at BBC headquarters who still considered the whole thing to be *a passing fad* and television programmes for many years yet took second place to BBC sound broadcasts with their audience of eleven and a half millions.

At Lime Grove the first studio to be opened was Studio D on the 4th floor which was equiped with three CPS Emitron cameras and was set aside for the children's television service.

21.5.1950 The first half-hour programme included a five minute episode of MUFFIN THE MULE. Annette Mills (sister of actor, John) had introduced Muffin first on August 4 1946 at Alexandra Palace and he was an established favourite. Annette told a musical story whilst seated at the piano, with Muffin on the piano top being manipulated by hidden puppeteer, Ann Hogarth. Included in the programme were Wilfred Pickles and Jimmy Hanley doing a paper tearing demonstration. Mrs Clement Attlee, the Prime Minister's lady opened the new studio and watched the programme.

Freda Lingstrom was the Head of the Department of Children's Television. Her qualifications for the post were nine years experience in sound school broadcasting. Working under her but in charge of all Childrens' programmes at Lime Grove was Cliff Michelmore. He was a free-lance sports commentator with sound broadcasting.

1951 He was warned that *Broadcasting House were not too keen on people deserting to television and that no one lasted for more than five years in children's television due to the ageing process.* However he *liked the idea of television and wanted to become involved there.* He spent a busy time travelling the country for his sports programmes whilst producing his children's programmes, which from September 1950 had increased to an hour each day. Until 1955 the BBC television service closed down between six and seven in the evening to enable mothers to get their children to bed! This was known as Toddler's Truce. Cliff Michelmore's first solo television production was at Freda Linstrom's suggestion, a programme on lacrosse, with a game performed in the cramped conditions at Alexandra Palace. In another programme from Lime Grove he explained the rules and scoring of tennis and introduced championship tennis from Wimbledon for children. A strong sports orientation. He said, *in those early days it was all improvisation – there would very often be ten minute gaps to fill, which meant a quick dash to the Science Museum to borrow an instructional model and the accompanying information on the development of the aeroplane, the paddlesteamer, or whatever.* From July 1950 he found he was spending more and more time at Lime Grove. There were no television instructors and no television training, you just watched and learnt as you went along. One thing Cliff Michelmore learned was that no children's programme was complete without *the ever present resident puppet.* Here are some of children's favourites from the 1950's. They were mainly aimed at the under sixes but I suspect had a broader following.

Muffin The Mule and Annette Mills. BBC

Jimmy Hanley. Gainsborough

Wilfred Pickles. John Vickers

Andy Pandy. Martin Grainger, Audrey Atterbury, Maria Bird and Janet Ferber. Peter H. Jones

1950-57 ANDY PANDY was a clown puppet created by Freda Lingstrom who wanted a programme for pre-school toddlers. She also wrote the scripts with Maria Bird who composed the music. Gladys Whitread sang the songs. The puppeteer was Audrey Atterbury, who says, *The first experimental programme was on June 20th 1950. This was not a great success as I was so nervous that I got the strings tangled up, went home, had a little weep and thought that's the end of that.*

However, it was the first of a very successful series and the early programmes were done live at Lime Grove. Later Andy Pandy was joined by Teddy and Looby Loo and Audrey by Molly Gibson. Occasionally Andy Pandy returned to Alexandra Palace. There were twenty six, 15 min episodes. It was included in WATCH WITH MOTHER on Tuesdays. Some new puppets by the same team appeared on Wednesdays in that programme from 1952-54.

BILL AND BEN, THE FLOWERPOT MEN were invented by Freda Lingstrom and made by Kim Allen. The scripts were by Freda Lingstrom and the music by Maria Bird who told the story.

96

The Puppeteers were Audrey Atterbury and Molly Gibson with the voices of Peter Hawkins and Gladys Whitread who was Little Weed. There were twenty six, 15 min episodes filmed at Lime Grove, Alexandra Palace and Kingswood Warren. Bill and Ben were favourites with the children but they spoke a Flowerpot language of their own. 'Oddle-poddle' which wasn't popular with the mothers who were teaching their children to speak correctly.

1954 THE PUPPET THEATRE was started in January and done live at Lime Grove in Studio E. It was produced by Ursula Eason with Freda Lingstrom. Various stories were enacted and programmes included Toytown and the Rubovia series, written and produced by Gordon Murray. Audrey Atterbury says, *In September 1955 we were allocated the tin shed at Lime Grove, which was literally that – a corrugated iron shed, for filming and rehearsing.*

BBC Puppet Theatre in Studio E. Clifford J. Matthews

The Tin Shed. Andrew Brainfoot, Noel Coleman, Maggie Ward, Peter Hawkins, Molly Gibson, Ivan Owen, Audrey Atterbury and John Hardwick.

97

1955-58 THE WOODENTOPS were created and scripted by Freda Lingstrom with help on the script from Maria Bird, who also wrote the music and told the story. The Puppeteers were Audrey Atterbury, Molly Gibson, Gordon Murray and others. The voices were Eileen Brown, Josephine Ray and Peter Hawkins. The Woodentops were an extended country family, including Buttercup the cow and Spotty Dog and shown on Fridays in WATCH WITH MOTHER.

The Wooden Tops

Harry Corbett, Sooty and Sweep

1953-55 RAG, TAG AND BOBTAIL were wild life characters and glove puppets manipulated by Sam and Elizabeth Williams on Thursdays.

1957 PINKY AND PERKY were imported Czech puppets.

1952 SOOTY made his debut on BBC television with the late Harry Corbett. Today Harry's son, Matthew, presents Sooty on Thames Television.

Valerie Hobson

Sylvia Peters. Picturegoer

Richard Hearne, Mr Pastry

Ian Carmichael

1.7.1951

In the early days it was not only ANDY PANDY who had a clowns face, Cliff Michelmore speaks of the *thick make-up applied to face and hands and arms in those days*. This under the heat of the lights too, but he said, *despite the privations, Lime Grove was where you had to be if you wanted to be part of this expanding, exciting service*. Not everyone felt like that, especially at Broadcasting House including the Director of Television himself, George Barnes. When cameraman, Don Gale asked the senior engineer if he could transfer from sound to television he was asked, *if he wanted to put his career in jeopardy, as television was only a passing fad, and would never catch on*. Television was still the Cinderella of the BBC. Some of the early children's programmes produced by Cliff Michelmore were PLAYBOX with Eamonn Andrews, who also joined the series early on as he *liked the idea of television*.

1950 TELESCOPE was a rather staid and educational magazine programme for children presented by Cliff Michelmore with Valerie Hobson in charge of the resident puppet, 'Timothy Telescope' and WHIRLIGIG which was *all jolly fun and games* and presented by Humphrey Lestocq. It went out fortnightly had its puppet 'Mr Turnip' and Steve Race at the piano, Rolf Harris made his first TV appearance on this show.

A children's sports programme was instigated and Cliff Michelmore introduced famous players like footballer Stanley Matthews and cricketer Dennis Compton. Richard Hearn's 'Mr Pastry' had worked in variety and comedy programmes on television as early as 1937. He appeared for the first time in a children's programme in August 1946. The character of 'Mr Pastry', complete with walrus moustache, flapping coat tails and hilarious dance routines, continued to amuse children in programmes as FOR THE CHILDREN 1946-50 and CRACKERJACK 1955-84. From 1950-51 he had his own programme, Mr PASTRY'S PROGRESS.

23.12.50 Light entertainment programmes moved into Studio G Lime Grove. One of the first programmes was, HERE'S TELEVISION written by Frank Muir and Dennis Norden, who developed into two of the stalwarts of television humour.

Ian Carmichael, who had appeared at Lime Grove as a film actor was now working as a free-lance television producer there in it's early days. He said of working at Lime Grove, *It was absolute heaven after Alexandra Palace. There was so much room. It was like Salisbury plain.*

IT'S A SMALL WORLD produced by Ian Carmichael. He described it as an early version of Spitting Image, using glove puppets and marionettes. It was not a success and despite the space there were many snags in Studio G. The cameras needed a lot of light and the heat from the lights sometimes caused the sprinklers to go off, soaking the set and everyone on it.

Gilbert Harding. BBC

Eamonn Andrews

Isobel Barnett. Delia Dudgeon

Elizabeth Allen

1947-53 CAFE CONTINENTAL produced by Henry Caldwell. This was first produced at Alexandra Palace in Studio A but transferred to Studio G, Lime Grove. It was a programme of cabaret acts which lasted 45 minutes and is remembered for its introduction and end. A handsome cab draws up at the entrance to the cafe and its occupants, the viewers, are ushered in by the doorman and greeted by Pere August. The diners then saw a number of spectacular acts. Josephine Baker appeared in an early programme. The Television Toppers, a dancing troupe, were often on the show. Finally the visitors were ushered into their cab and as it left the blind on the back window was pulled down announcing 'The End'. It was 'corny' but it has proved memorable.

Ronnie Waldman, formerly of sound radio, was Head of Light Entertainment and in searching for suitable material was offered a panel game established in America which he thought worth a try. Sold to the BBC for 25 Guineas a programme, it was:-

7.1951 WHAT'S MY LINE The panel of four had to try and discover the occupations of the guests and were helped by a mime. Ronnie Waldman considered as possible Chairman, Eamonn Andrews or Gilbert Harding. They were each given a trial but owing to one of Gilbert's shows of temperament (always fascinating to the viewers) Eamonn was chosen but Gilbert Harding was included in the panel. Others were, Barbara Kelly, actress; Ted Kavanagh, ITMA scriptwriter; Marghanita Laski, writer; and Jerry Desmonde, comedian. In time others replaced them, including David Nixon, Isobel Barnett, Elizabeth Allen, and Michael Dennison. In all What's My Line ran for twelve years with two revivals on other channels. Many other quizzes were tried through the years, but none was quite as successful. Eamonn proved a skilled chairman with the knack of keeping panelists and challengers happy. Given the list of competitors he studied the professions meticulously before the show. Much of its attraction came from the iracible Gilbert Harding. The studio audience and viewers waited for his outbursts of irritability. There seemed to be a battle of wits between him and Eamonn but in reality they had a healthy respect for one another. Gilbert Harding, a well known radio voice, very literate and cultivated, was one of the first television 'stars'. *He had the air of a stern headmaster and his friends suggested he was wasting his talents on a simple panel game, but Gilbert had no high opinion of his ability and was even embarrassed at the amount of money he received for appearing.* It was Gilbert, growling and pedantic, the viewers turned on to see, hoping for a clash between him and a challenger, the chairman or a panelist! They did try him with his own programme, HARDING FINDS OUT but it was not a success.

There was also a fascination with the lady panelist's long dangley earings, Barbara Kelly's at first and later Isobel Barnett's. Necklines were important and a change of hairstyle brought many letters from the public, they were the first television superstars. Gilbert Harding died in 1960 and the show lost much of its sparkle. When it was revived on BBC in 1973-4 it had 7,000,000 viewers.

Isobel Barnett presented one of the first consumer programmes LOOK AND CHOOSE and received an award for it as *Television's Top Women Personality*. She always likened her visits to Lime Grove to *visits to the dentist. People might say 'relax' it will be alright but it was untrue.* If performers resorted to alcohol to strengthen their nerves it and the heat of the lights reduced them to a torpor.

Charlie Chester

Benny Hill

Peter Ustinov. Tom Blau, Camera Press

Terry Thomas

Light entertainment included many shows built around popular comedians such as:-

1951-5 THE CHARLIE CHESTER SHOW produced by Walton Anderson and written by 'Cheerful Charlie' who appeared with Arthur Haynes, Deryck Guyler and guests.

1952 THE HOWERD CROWD produced by Bill Lyon Shaw with scripts by Eric Sykes, an hour long programme presenting Frankie Howerd in his first television series.

1953 IN ALL DIRECTIONS with Peter Ustinov and Peter Jones.

1953 TAKE IT EASY the first of many shows starring Norman Wisdom.

1953-55 BEFORE YOUR VERY EYES produced by Bill Ward. A fortnightly 30 min series starring Arthur Askey with Dickie Henderson and Diana Decker.

THIS IS SHOW BUSINESS with Vic Oliver.

HOW DO YOU VIEW? with Terry Thomas.

Benny Hill made his first appearance at this time.

THE HIT PARADE appeared once a month, a forerunner of TOP OF THE POPS (1964) which sometimes came from Lime Grove.

1950 A MATTER OF LIFE AND DEATH was one of the first medical programmes.

1950 A programme was transmitted across the Channel for the first time RELAY FROM CALAIS on 28.8.1950.

1952 PARIS PANORAMA transmitted on 14.7.1952 from Paris and hosted by Richard Dimbleby and Sylvia Peters was a magazine programme including a visit to the Louvre, a fashion show and a military tattoo. A special convertor was needed to change from French definition standards to British and the images were carried over radio links in eight stages.

1950 THE OXFORD AND CAMBRIDGE BOAT RACE was an outstanding early outside broadcast using for the first time a television camera mounted on the following launch. There were also twelve cameras mounted at points on the shore all linked to Lime Grove.

1952 When King George VI died suddenly in February, the television service closed down for forty eight hours. When programmes recommenced Eric Robinson, Musical Director, put together a show of light classical music and ballet for the first time presenting it himself. From this evolved:-

1952-9 MUSIC FOR YOU produced by Patricia Foy and presented by Eric Robinson which was a pot-pourri of classical works with great performers like Moiseiwitch. Some ballet was included. It was very popular with the public but a nightmare for the programme makers when great operatic stars were included, as they arrived on the day of the show and with a live show, all their demands, lateness and temperament had to be ironed out shortly before they appeared.

9.9.55 MUSIC AT TEN presented by Eric Robinson featured Alicia Markova in Act II of Giselle. In the following month Les Sylphide was performed with Nina Vyroubova, the Ballet Rambert and a section of the Royal Opera House Orchestra conducted by John Hollingsworth.

Usually Eric Robinson conducted and presented the popular ballets and leading performers of the time.

1956 Christmas Day In MUSIC FOR YOU, Eric Robinson presented a Christmas feast with Joan Hammond, Ferruccio Tagliavini, Anneliese Rothenberger, Larry Adler, Eileen Joyce, Marcel Cornelius, Jose Greco, and Beryl Grey, with the Ballet Rambert in Les Sylphide. The programme began at 10.00 pm and lasted an hour and a quarter.

Anne Ziegler

Thelma Lister in Coppelia

Music For You 5.9.1956. Eileen Joyce and The Royal Philharmonic Orchestra.

A member of Shepherd's Bush local history society, Thelma Lister, danced with the Ballet Rambert at Lime Grove on many occasions between 1953 and 1959. She says, *The Christmas Day transmissions were fun to do and working at Lime Grove was quite an experience.* Thelma also remembers that 'big' names were handled with care and confirms that some could be temperamental and cites Anne Ziegler of the singing partnership, Anne Ziegler and Webster Booth as being quite a handful.

Childrens television had its own 'soap':-

1952-57 THE APPLEYARDS which told of the ups and downs in a family's life. There were eleven series with 20 min episodes.

'The Evening Standard' on the 3rd of December 1951 showed some of the thirty five entrants who were auditioning for the part of:-

BILLY BUNTER OF GREYFRIARS SCHOOL produced by Joy Harrington. Gerald Campion was the finalist and suitably rotund to suggest Bunter's absolute preoccupation with food. The stories by Frank Richards first appeared in the pre-1914 comic 'The Magnet'. The series in half-hour episodes lasted for ten years.

There was one outside broadcast which was responsible for a great increase in the television sets in public use and that was:-

1953 THE CORONATION OF QUEEN ELIZABETH I I on June 2nd.

There were an estimated 20,000,000 viewers in the UK alone. Brighton had been out of television range until this time, however this programme was relayed to France, Belgium, Holland and West Germany. Telefilms reached Canada that evening and film was processed in flight to New York in specially chartered Canberra bombers, to be shown the same evening. Five Regional transmitters covered about 84% of the population of Britain, a higher proportion than in any other country. The transmission lasted from 10.15 am until 5.20 pm. The Coronation service in Westminster Abbey was described by Richard Dimbleby who was there throughout the whole event, seventeen hours.

Television had arrived. The topic of conversation on the commuter trains became what had been seen on television the previous evening. Television tables and chairs, dishes and dinners arrived and a forest of television aerials sprang up.

30.11.1953 The new Queen and Prince Philip made their first visit to Lime Grove. The red carpet was rolled out and a rare outside event was the bestowing of a knighthood on George Barnes, Director of Television. The ceremonial sword was brought from Buckingham Palace. Cecil Madden, programme organiser and senior producer gave his office for the ceremony. It was converted into *a sort of Palm Court.* A dias was built in the studio with chairs from the property department, hastily painted gold. Queen Elizabeth saw a play THE DISAGREEABLE MAN and an all star variety show FOR YOUR PLEASURE. The stars were Norman Wisdom, Terry Thomas, Al Read, Jimmy Edwards, David Nixon and the Television Toppers. Pat Kirkwood sang *My Old Man Said Follow the Van* in her portrayal of Marie Lloyd which she had performed earlier that year in OUR MARIE with great success.

During the show Sir George Barnes' chair collapsed under him and he was left sitting on the floor. The Queen looked apprehensively at her own chair, as well she might as many of the chairs were later found to be rotten.

Cliff Michelmore and the author. Richard Sadler

Studio plan 1951

Lime Grove could put on a show in those days, apart from transmissions. There was a team of magnificently uniformed commissionaires, led by Harold Stacey with five page boys in navy suits and Eton collars. They were certainly needed to guide people through *the hotchpotch of corridors, studios and hospitality rooms.* Lime Grove studios were visited by so many celebrities in its time. All the Prime Ministers of Britain, from Anthony Eden, to Margaret Thatcher, came there to record the crisis of the time. Anthony Eden rehearsing his speech in a quiet corner was mistaken for an escaped lunatic by a zealous employee. King Hussein of Jordan, the Aga Khan and President Eisenhower came. When Vice President Hubert Humphrey came to appear on PANORAMA, his twenty security men were so zealous they found Robin Day's dirty shirts in his briefcase, although Joan Marsden had assured them there was nothing dangerous there. Woodrow Wyatt and Senator Nixon also appeared on PANORAMA. The artists included famous international stars like Maria Callas, The Bolshei Ballet and Louis Armstrong. Bing Crosby and Frank Sinatra appeared on IN TOWN TONIGHT. Princess Anne and Prince Charles visited as children and as they grew up. Princess Margaret hummed 'Lizzie Borden' to Ronnie Waldman while she watched THE TIN PAN ALLEY SHOW in Studio G's control box.

1961 The Queen celebrated twenty five years of television by watching an edition of CRACKERJACK. Eamonn Andrews presented her with two silver propelling pencils for Prince Charles and Princess Anne but forgot Prince Andrew's name. The Queen covered for him by accepting the Andy Pandy doll *for the little one Mr Andrews? Yes Ma'am* said a relieved Eamonn.

21.8.53 Studio E came into commission and this was the home of the large drama and light entertainment productions which drew the biggest audiences. Michael Mills produced the first programme in Studio E and was so impressed with the space after the cramped conditions of Alexandra Palace he had Bill Fraser drive in a sports car just to show how much room there was. Despite the space Peter Black says, *Nobody could make a television play a comfortable thing to do. The early equipment taxed those on both sides of the camera to the limit. The dazzle and heat of the arc lights were intense enough to cook Philip Harben's omelette before he got it in the pan.* In the summer Lime Grove became unbearable.

Producing plays or any programme with cameras that moved like tanks in terrific heat, with no video recorders or teleprompters seems an impossible task. Everyone however has a great affection for the days of live television despite its privations. Michael Mills remembers *the effect of everyone working so close to one another in such difficulties made for a tremendous camaraderie.* There would be an Ibsen play one day and a variety show the next. There were no dummy runs, everything was tried out live in full view of the public.

Added to production difficulties material was limited. Many suitable books for adaptation were under contract to the cinema or theatre, both very jealous of television's influence. BBC sound radio, for the same reason was eager to keep plays and players under contract to them for their own audience. The Classics including Shakespeare and Dickens were available. The first series of SHERLOCK HOLMES had been shown in 1951 to coincide with the Sherlock Holmes Exhibition in Baker Street for The Festival of Britain.

Peter Cushing

6.12.1953 WUTHERING HEIGHTS was adapted by Nigel Kneale with Richard Todd and Yvonne Mitchell. It was produced by Rudolph Cartier.
Actors found the television studios so difficult anyway few wished to transfer from the theatre and audiences, to the terrors of live performances. Plays had to be edited to remove changes of costume and scene which couldn't be accomplished easily on the stages. The budgets were extremely small as the limited number of viewers in proportion to listeners to sound radio who paid the licences, didn't warrant it. Because of this actors in television were paid only two thirds of radio actor's fees. Authors were paid by the minute as in sound radio. The actors being more confident in a repeat got through the programme quicker and the author was surprised to find he got less for the second performance.
Cecil Madden had established the principle of Sunday Night Drama with a repeat on Thursday evening as long ago as March 1938. There were many excellent productions in the early 50's but one was outstanding it was another adaptation by Nigel Kneale.
12.12.1954 1984 by George Orwell. Peter Cushing played Winston Smith and Yvonne Mitchell was Julia. The live presentation lasted 120 minutes and was produced by Rudolph Cartier who had onced worked in Germany with Max Reinhardt and lived in the glory of those days. He was often heard to say, *I shall need a hundred extras for this.* He didn't get them but his maxim *one only discovers the possibilities of television by attempting the impossible* worked wonders. The budget for props for 1984 was £50 and with that, amazing gadgets were put together in the visual effects department. After the Sunday night showing there were many complaints from viewers, especially about the rats. Newspaper headlines next day read, TORTURES ON TV HORRIFY WHOLE NATION. MP's tried to ban the repeat. Peter Cushing's torture by rats was the controversial subject. Genuine sewer rats had been tried out at first but they passed out with the heat of the lamps. Two white rats were obtained from a local pet shop and coloured up with Leichner No.3. When Christine Hillcoat in Make-up was asked for the colour she thought she was being usurped but declined the job when she saw the rats. The rats were kept in and the programme went out on Thursday but there were very few complaints the second time. The furore had died down, videotape had just arrived and the second showing was taped but Peter Cushing said *it lacked the spontaneity of the first performance.* He like the pet shop rats managed to survive the terrors of Studio E but he said he *never lost his dread of a television performance.* He did numerous productions on television, at one time at a rate of one a month, and became a well-known household face. He won The National Television Award for *Outstanding Actor of the Year 1953-54* and The Guild of TV Producers and Directors awarded him *Best Performance Award for '1984'.* One production had the distinction of being created for television and then being taken up by the theatre and made into a film by Alfred Hitchcock, it was:-
1952 DIAL M FOR MURDER a play by Frederick Knott.
In a lighter vein, Michael Mills produced some memorable productions, like the:-
1953 THE PASSING SHOWS which consisted of five 100 min programmes telling the history of popular entertainment in the first half of the century. They were very elaborate and fast moving and there were as many as 105 sets per programme. The sets were used, taken down and replaced while the action of the play was going on. Sometimes the props

Lime Grove Studios. Photowork

Lime Grove Studios 1990

The Shepherd's Bush Empire 1918. W. Straker

department which was in the old Studio F was completely full of scenery for just one episode. In OUR MARIE*, Pat Kirkwood had numerous costume changes, all during the action of the play, that alone must have been exhausting. A special dressing room was built amongst the props for her quick changes. She stripped and dressed as she ran from Studio E to F and back again. It was one song from this sequence which was chosen for the Royal Visit. Another episode was the story of C.B. Cochran and his 'Young Ladies'.   (*The story of Marie Lloyd.) Another tremendous hit at the time was a serial written by Nigel Kneale:-

1953 THE QUATERMASS EXPERIMENT with Reginal Tate as the Professor and Duncan Lamont as Victor Carroon. There were six episodes of 30 min each. It was an early science fiction serial which told of the lone survivor of a rocket crew who mutated into an enormous vegetable-like creature. The entire television audience became housebound when the episodes were being shown. A second series of six episodes of 30 min were shown:-

1955 QUARTERMASS II with John Robinson as Professor Quatermass was also done at Lime Grove but two further series were not. The producer was the clever and flamboyant Rudolph Cartier. Jack King was the modelmaker for the series.

The old film Studio F was used exclusively for scenery and props in immediate use so that they could be wheeled onto the set in quick succession. There were other storage rooms for props from costumes to furniture. Frank Holland, Property Master catalogued all props on a system probably still used. A system was needed as earlier there were hiccups. The Gas Board once enquired, *if the twenty five gas cookers on loan to Lime Grove were still all needed?* Frank Holland on looking into the store found there were twenty five all marked N.T.G.B. (North Thames Gas Board) which had been interpreted as Not to Go Back!

A request came to him once for a desk for a French period play complete with quill pens and French letters. A note went back to the Drama Department to say *if the last item was correspondence they could supply them but otherwise they were the responsibility of the Costume Department.* There were definite divisions. Trained animals came under Artists Contracts, untrained Props Dept.

Frank Holland sent Jimmy Whigham out once to get twenty copies each of 'The Evening News', 'The Evening Standard' and 'The Star' from outside Shepherd's Bush tube station. Before he got to the tube he came upon a newspaper-seller and placed his order, he got the reply *Piss off, this is the bloody filming.*

The drama programmes of the early fifties included all the classic adventures from Robin Hood and The Scarlet Pimpernel to The Three Musketeers. From Peter Cushing as Beau Brummel to Alfie Bass in The Bespoke Overcoat. For the children Worzel Gummidge to The Children of the New Forest. Sherwood Forest and The New Forest were all created in the studio, and it was hoped the action travelled smoothly from set to set. In The Children of the New Forest the budget didn't allow for two armies so roundheads did a quick change and became cavaliers.

A prompter was invented by which the sound was blotted out for a moment whilst the actor was prompted. An elderly actor said to another, *don't worry old boy if you 'dry' just carry on mouthing words and they'll think its a technical fault and they've lost the sound,* tells Christine Hillcoat. June Whitfield says, *if you got through those early programmes without a piece of*

Norman Wisdom, Jerry Desmonde, Jill Day, Eamonn Andrews, Yvonne Mitchell and Larry Adler.

Frank Muir

Denis Norden. Thames Television

scenery falling on you, you were lucky. If the worse came to the worse the sign, NORMAL SERVICE WILL BE RESUMED AS SOON AS POSSIBLE was displayed.

A troup of dancers covered a scene change in a musical show. There were always THE INTERLUDES. These covered any disaster and kept the viewer in a relaxed mood until the programme was resumed. A potter's wheel, a kitten playing with a ball of wool, a slowly turning windmill, a fish swimming in a tank, were some of them.

Equipment which seemed to break down more than most was the PASSENGER LIFT. Once when it was out of order Golda Meir, Prime Minister of Israel and Richard Dimbleby climbed to the fourth floor for an interview. She was so out of breath that Richard Dimbleby had to do most of the talking at first until she got her breath back. It plummeted once with four Commonwealth Prime Ministers inside. Paul Fox was once stuck with Jomo Kenyatta, and his bodyguards.

The building seems to have had its drawbacks too. Cliff Michelmore *calls it a mess of a building, a disastrous mess.* The contracters Robert Hart employed a full time man just to maintain the hundreds of doors in the studios. Frank Muir in his own inimitable style says, *Lime Grove could not possibly have been built for anything except the engine room of the Queen Elizabeth. My prevailing memory of it, was getting lost. You would keep meeting the same people every few minutes in the corridors, all looking for different rooms, and no matter what time you arrived you only reached the studio in the nick of time. I'm convinced that's why the programmes always seemed so full of life because everyone was hot and out of breath.*

Once a French singer in CAFE CONTINENTAL threw a fit of temper and left the studio. Henry Caldwell tried to calm him down whilst conducting him on a circular tour of the building and by the time they 'inadvertently' reached the studio again things had calmed down.

Despite everything the programmes rolled out.

WHAT'S MY LINE had been such a hit that there had always been a search for other panel games which would be as successful. Many were launched, FIND THE LINK; THE NAMES THE SAME with a panel comprising Frank Muir, Dennis Norden, Katie Boyle and Brenda Bruce; WHAT DO YOU KNOW?, GUESS MY STORY; WHOSE BABY? etc. few lasted.

1952-59 ANIMAL, VEGETABLE, MINERAL was a fortnightly quiz which did become popular and ran for seven years. A panel of experts had to identify an unusual object chosen from a museum collection. Chaired by Glyn Daniel it had a panel of distinguished academicians including Sir Mortimer Wheeler who went on to later present his own programmes, **THE GRANDEUR THAT WAS ROME; GREECE** etc. produced by Stephen Hurst. Fascinating programmes on archaeology. Another panelist obviously chosen for his name was Professor Thomas Bodkin.

1955-61 THE BRAINS TRUST was produced by Peter Brook and directed by John Furness. A popular wartime radio favourite this programme came to television. The questions which viewers wanted to know were put to some of the most eminnent brains of the time. The original question master was Hugh Ross Williamson. The panelists had no prior knowledge of the questions and the answers were spontaenous which made for a lively programme.

Peter Woods. BBC

McDonald Hobley. BBC

Robert Dougall. BBC

The twenty five gas cookers were probably left over from the numerous cookery demonstrations which were always popular.

1950 THE CRADOCKS with Johnnie and Fanny Cradock, a husband and wife team. Their programmes continued through to 1975. They had their own unique brand of cookery and I'm sure much of their fascination was, that viewers hoped one day to see Johnnie crown Fanny with a rolling pin. Jeff the Chef in the BBC Club Sandwich Bar always put on an act of furiously sharpening the carving knife when Fanny came into the Club.

1950-56 COOKERY LESSON was demonstrated by Philip Harben who first appeared on television in 1946 when ration books were still in use. He appeared in various series until 1969. They were all usually afternoon programmes.

Cookery seems to create great television personalities from Graham Kerr to our present Floyd and Loyd.

1953-61 ASIAN CLUB distinguished guest speakers like Bertrand Russell discussed problems with a studio audience.

1953 DEATH OF A TOWN an impressive documentary of the Greek earthquake by Kay Cicelliss.

1954-61 ZOO QUEST was the first programme produced by David Attenborough at Lime Grove. He became a star overnight when a baby chimpanzee frightened by the studio lights clung around his neck.

David Attenborough said, *there were only half a dozen of us doing the whole of non-fiction television. Sometimes two or three programmes a week.* He recalls, *Lime Grove was a real dynamo. When you had programmes on Christmas Day people went in to do them. Christmas Day at Lime Grove was fun.* Audrey Atterbury said much the same thing about Alexandra Palace where she had to take her small boy if she was working on Christmas Day. Paul is now a television star himself on The Antiques Road Show. With pre-recordings Christmas Day parties at White City must be dull affairs.

1952 Studio H was the smallest, and used first in February 1952 when the 'Talks' department moved there from Alexandra Palace. The EMI camera installed there was idiosyncratic and if the light intensity increased suddenly it gave a simulated explosion on the screen, so it needed much care.

On one occasion a children's play was squeezed in, it was HEIDI with Julia Lockwood (daughter of Margaret). Space was so limited that one of the goats ate the floor manager's shooting script and the programme had to go out live without it.

TALKS was a title from sound radio meaning an illustrated talk, soon to be changed to CURRENT AFFAIRS.

1948-54 THE BBC TELEVISION NEWSREEL had been produced by Harold Cox, ex-Gaumont British, since 1948. The 15 min programmes followed the newsreel pattern and gave a summary of the week's news.

1951 WEEKEND NEWS REVIEW was shown on Sundays and gave selected items from the week's news. Richard Dimbleby was the linkman.

Richard Dimbleby, Voice Of The Nation. BBC

Richard Dimbleby, having his hands cast at Madam Tussauds. Madam Tussauds

117

29.3.1953 The first live television news bulletin was shown strictly according to the rules laid down at Broadcasting House *to state the news of the day accurately, fairly, soberly and impersonally.* There was no newscaster shown. Broadcasting House thought *television newsreels would never replace news on sound* and John Snagg *thought news readers would be a distraction on television.* So that headlines were read after the evening's programmes. Here are the programmes for a day in February 1955.

Programmes began at 3.00 pm.

3.00	FAMILY AFFAIRS Produced by Michael Mills
3.30	IN TOWN TONIGHT
4.00	WATCH WITH MOTHER
5.00	CHILDRENS TELEVISION
6.00	Toddlers Truce
7.25	WEATHER
7.30	NEWS
7.40	PORTRAIT OF ALISON – thriller, Episode 3.
8.15	TELEVISION TIME
9.00	VIEWFINDER
9.30	VIEW CLUES – Crossword Game
9.45	LOOK AT IT THIS WAY – Eric Barker
10.15	SCIENCE REVIEW
10.30	NEWS (sound only)

One channel only in black and white and when a motor cyclist went by you saw only a 'snowstorm'! However commercial television was coming. They couldn't afford a Toddlers Truce when time was money. They were to have personality newscasters and presenters like Chris Chataway, Robin Day, Ludovic Kennedy and Reginald Bosanquet.

There had to be changes. Things hummed at Lime Grove, the service expanded and new exciting programmes were planned. The Head of Department was Leonard Miall and he was fortunate in having as his head assistant, a small formidable woman, Grace Wyndham-Goldie. She *had one of the most original minds in the BBC hierarchy. She influenced all the non-fiction productions vigoroulsly propelling them towards innovation and expansion.* Charles de Jaeger. She gathered around her a brilliant team who brought about the changes needed.

Donald Baverstock *had a flair for a topical story, he was clever and widely read.* Alasdair Milne was another. Two years after joining the BBC as a trainee he was at Lime Grove in the Talks department and went on to become Director General of the BBC. This talent was needed to keep the BBC ahead of the new commercial channels. The service expanded and five regional studios came into being.

1955 PANORAMA was re-vamped with Richard Dimbleby as its presenter. Newscasters appeared and regular news bulletins for the first time. Also HIGHLIGHT was introduced.

Vice President Hubert Humphrey

Brigitte Bardot

Gene Kelly

Arthur Askey

1955 HIGHLIGHT was an innovative programme, produced by Donald Baverstock. It was only an early evening 10 min one. It was made in Studio P which was a tiny backstairs studio with only enough room for two cameras, a microphone and three chairs. The interviewers were Cliff Michelmore and Geoffry Johnson-Smith. The latter once interviewed Brigitte Bardot, beauty and animal lover, who spoke of her *naughty little dog who goes pee-pee all over the flat.* Studio P became Studio PP from then on. Its other claim to fame was that it was the studio where Anthony Eden made his historic Suez announcement.

The subjects to be covered were *anything that will interest or disturb us and by definition the viewer.* HIGHLIGHT was the precursor to TONIGHT. It was a new kind of television journalism. *The old fashioned deferential conservative style was out and colloquial language was in.* The whole style of television interviewing was changed. *We ask sensible relevant questions and look for sensible relevant answers* said Donald Baverstock. Saturday sport was included.

STUDIO P was in Smith's Yard. It was designed as a continuity studio for announcers but gradually got used for small programmes for already the studios were outgrowing the space. At this time the staff had reached one thousand and every space in the main building was utilised for cutting, editing and dubbing rooms. The BBC rented terrace houses in Lime Grove and other streets nearby. Public Halls in Shepherd's Bush were used as rehearsal rooms and caravans were parked between buildings for use as offices.

SMITH'S YARD also had various departments in it, including in 'Smiths Buildings' editing and film despatch.

But the most important was the BBC CLUB, a temporary looking structure but *more money was taken over the counter here in a lunchtime than in all the surrounding pubs put together.* Here the programme bosses met at lunch time and after work to gossip, conspire and plan. The Beatles visited it once. Cliff Michelmore tells how Tony Hancock came to see TONIGHT go out from the control gallery. He was shocked and amazed at the character shredding and self criticism that went on afterwards at the BBC Club but he thought it marvellous that they did it. *We ought to do that after our programmes. All we do is tell each other how good we are.*

There was also some coveted car parking spaces and Sue Lawley says, *You had 'arrived' when you got your space there.*

The doyen of all commentators was Richard Dimbleby. He started in sound radio and was a war correspondent. His television experience included the first major outside broadcasts, THE VICTORY PARADE 1946; THE LONDON OLYMPICS 1948; THE GENERAL ELECTION 1950; THE RELAY FROM CALAIS 1950; PARIS PANORAMA 1952; THE CORONATION 1953 and much more. Cliff Michelmore says, *Richard was unique, a man of his time who set standards he expected the rest of us to follow. His preparation for any broadcast was meticulous and his presentation faultless.* He was a national institution "the voice of the Nation". Listeners and viewers recognised his quiet, unflapable style immediately. He was a master of his craft. He noted his prompts on little cards. Cliff Michelmore followed his method. Eamonn Andrews worked from a script which was fraught with dangers when some improvisation or minor disaster occurred, which they did. Jack Warner as George Dixon noted his prompts on PC Andy Crawford's (Peter Byrne) station desk pad. Actors in long dramas pinned their prompt cards to the scenery.

Richard Dimbleby with his method and intensive homework never faltered in his commentaries.

Richard Baker reader of first TV News 5.7.54.

James Burke

Peter Haigh presenter Picture Parade 1956-62 with Josephine Douglas presenter and co-producer Six-Five Special 1957-58.

He was always a free-lance and stayed with PANORAMA until his death. When given news of his illness viewers and friends sent 7,000 letters to the hospital.

1953-1990 PANORAMA is the oldest established current affairs programme on television. It began as a lightly topical programme with book, theatre and art reviews and went out fortnightly (1953), but when Richard Dimbleby headed the team from 1955 it became weekly and then nightly. Once established it was considered the most powerful and respected television programme of its type, "A Window on the World". The editorial executives were Grace Wyndham-Goldie and Paul Fox and the 1950's team were Chris Chataway and John Freeman and the 1960's team Michael Barratt, Robin Day, Michael Charlton, Trevor Phipott and Leonard Parkin. The programme always had an eminent list of presenters. It had the distinction of being ordered off the screen by Winston Churchill. This was when President Makarios of Cyprus was interviewed and condoned the action against the British. However the programme continued and had many other notable guests. King Hussein of Jordan in 1959 and an exclusive interview with President Kennedy by Ludovic Kennedy on the Radziwill's doorstep, whilst on a private visit to Britain.

My favourite incident is a visit paid by Dag Hammarskjold. It was usual to do a rehearsal before the show, with anyone who was handy, sitting in for the 'stars' Albert Stevenson, a light entertainments producer took the chair. The interviewer, Francis Williams asked, *Tell me Mr Hammarskjold, how did you come to be appointed Secretary General of the United Nations.* Albert replied, *Well I was unemployed at the time, and as I was walking down the road one day this geezer comes up to me and says How'd you like to be Secretary General of the United Nations?* Grace Wyndham Goldie who was in the gallery 'tore him off a strip'. Also concealed in the studio was Dag Hammarskjold who when he took his seat and was asked the question still in rehearsal he replied, *well I was walking down the street and this geezer came up to me.* etc. etc. all this in a Swedish-cockney accent. I love this story as in my experience most Swedes don't always have such a quick sense of humour!

April 1st 1957
The most memorable programme for the majority was when Richard Dimbleby showed the annual Spaghetti harvest in Lugano Italy. It was being gathered off the trees by girls on ladders and in National dress. It was an April Fool's Day spoof dreamed up by cameraman, Charles de Jaeger. With great difficulty his team had hung strands of cooked spaghetti on the laurel hedge of a Lugano Hotel and filmed the girls filling their baskets. Not everyone realised the joke!

The PANORAMA office was in what had been an attic bedroom of one of the terraced houses adjoining the studios. The BBC bought three houses but one tenant living in the middle of the three refused to sell and cultivated his garden and lived we hope, happily with the PANORAMA office on one side and QUESTION TIME on the other. Meanwhile producers made tortuous journies from the main block, up and down stairs across an open area and through a backdoor. No wonder that finding an office was considered a sort of initiative test in getting a post at Lime Grove. If you found the office you got the job.

Percy Thrower. Carl and Pat Jameson.

Gardening Club 1955-67. The Roof Garden. Percy Thrower advising Mr D.E.P. Dunne and Mr R.C. Balfour on the winter storing of vegetables. BBC Photograph Library

There had been gardening programmes at Alexandra Palace, and they had had a demonstration gardening plot. At Lime Grove it was on the roof. There was a greenhouse, tubs and hanging baskets. Salads, flowers and other crops were grown in the highest garden in Shepherd's Bush, seven stories above the pavement for:-

14.1.1955-67 GARDENING CLUB presented by Percy Thrower.
A replica greenhouse was built in the studio and the plants were brought down for the transmission. Percy Thrower gave gardening information and introduced guests to the programme from gardening societies. Demonstrations were filmed on the roof.

1955-67 LOOK Sir Peter Scott presented this early wildlife programme.
Previously on 22.1.54 Sir Peter released a wild mallard duck from the roof of Lime Grove studios bound for his 'Severn Wild Life Trust' reserve at Slimbridge, Gloucestershire. According to the local paper it landed instead at 71 Stowe Road, Shepherd's Bush and was taken to the RSPCA who released it in St. James Park next morning.
At least two people committed suicide by jumping off the roof during the BBC's tenure. In both cases personal problems were given as the reason not pressure of work.

1954-5 WAR IN THE AIR was produced and written by John Elliot. Narrated by Robert Harris and with special music composed by Sir Arthur Bliss, Master of the Queen's Music.
A documentary series telling the story of power in the air. There were fifteen half hour films.

1955 ITS MAGIC presented by David Nixon, magician and entertainer.
A programme of illusion which was the forerunner of many since.

1956-60 FRONTIERS OF SCIENCE was a popular science programme produced by James McCloy.

1957 THE SKY AT NIGHT has been presented by Dr. Patrick Moore for nearly forty years. The programme began six months before the launching of Sputnik I and Patrick Moore has guided us through the astronomical events of the years with his breezy manner ever since. He succeeds in explaining the infinite to us all.

1969 In APOLLO James Burke and Patrick Moore reported man's first landing on the moon and answered children's questions. Other features at this time were:-

1956-62 PICTURE PARADE presented by Peter Haigh and Derek Bond, which was an early weekly magazine programme about the cinema and the new releases. Robert Robinson took over in 1959 and Barry Norman from 1972.

1956-68 ZOO TIME with Desmond Morris consisted of 331 half hour editions. It was mainly based at London Zoo but Lime Grove studios were no strangers to wild animals. Anthony Smith when part of the Talks Department was incarcerated in the lift with a lion. Once the lions from Bertram Mills Circus were roaming Smith's Yard.
One day Ronnie Waldman invited Leslie Jackson to a small studio in Lime Grove to watch another American show. They both thought it had popular appeal and that proved to be the case for it ran from 1955-1964 on BBC and still continues today on Thames Television. It was

29.7.1955 THIS IS YOUR LIFE produced by Leslie Jackson with Eamonn Andrews as Master of Ceremonies. In it some unsuspecting celebrity was accosted by Eamonn and presented with a large red book labelled 'This is Your Life'. This part was always pre-filmed. They were then taken to the studio and forced to endure the public recreation of their lives through surprise guests from the past. It could produce some very emotional reunions and it

Jessie Matthews

Bernard Braden. Associated Television

Derek Bond

Jimmy Edwards

has been accused of trading on cheap emotions. But the viewers love it. In 1958 Anna Neagle had broken down in torrents of tears and others suffered similarly.

The victim had to be lured to the studio or venue, on some pretext and it had to be kept a secret from them as surprise was the main element. If the news was 'leaked' as it was with Stanley Matthews, who was to have been the subject of the first show, someone else had to be substituted at short notice. It took months to prepare the programmes and contact the surprise guests. With Stanley Matthews declared void, Eamonn was told that Freddie Mills, the boxer, was to be substituted. Eamonn thought, that Freddie thought, he was to appear as a panelist on a sports quiz programme. Eamonn had dinner with Freddie and sat next to him in the studio audience. At 7.45 pm the programme began and the presenter, Ralph Edwards, moved among the audience. Eamonn smiled confidently but when the book was handed to him, he realised the subterfuge and said, *Oh blimey!* He was dazed but carried on through the half hour programme, smiling but becoming tearful when his mother appeared.

When another footballer, Danny Blanchflower was presented with the red book *'This is Your Life'* he said, *Oh no its not!* and went out of the studio door. He said later he, *just disliked the nature of the programme and as it happened I hated at least a third of the people who were supposed to come on and say nice things about me. It would have been hypocritical if I had pretended I was glad to see them.* Many other people disliked the programme or Eamonn's style and let it be known they never wished to appear. The viewers loved it. Eamonn did 900 episodes in over thirty years and his friendly manner made the show a success.

1961 Jessie Matthews received a telephone call from the BBC inviting her back to Lime Grove to be a mystery guest celebrity on WHAT'S MY LINE on the Sunday evening of the 26th March she arrived at Lime Grove studios in a limousine and was met by Eamonn Andrews who said, *Jessie Matthews, tonight, This is Your Life. Please no, you mustn't do this* she said. However she calmed down and agreed to do it and a pleasantly diluted version of her life unfolded. There was no reference to her first and third husbands and only a brief mention of Sonnie Hale. Her adopted daughter refused to appear saying, *I'm afraid I find programmes of that sort dreadfully vulgar.* She was in a minority for the programme which first appeared once a month was so popular it became weekly.

Light entertainment at this time included:-

1954 EVENING AT HOME with Bernard Braden and Barbara Kelly and was an early domestic comedy series.

1954-7 THE GROVE FAMILY was the first television 'soap' serial it paid tribute to the street in which it was made in its title.

1955-6 LIFE WITH THE LYONS a fortnightly series produced by Bryan Sears.

Bebe Daniels and Ben Lyon had come to television via Hollywood and the radio show HI GANG! A feature film of which was made by Gainsborough at Lime Grove in 1941. This was a family sitcom featuring real life family, Bebe and Ben and their children Barbara and Richard.

1956-60 and **1971-2** WHACK-O! with scripts by Frank Muir and Dennis Norden featuring Jimmy Edwards. This situation comedy is legendary. Jimmy Edwards played the infamous headmaster of Chiselbury Public School. Arthur Howard played his simple-minded assistant, Mr Pettigrew and there was an assortment of awful boys.

Billy Cotton

Alma Cogan

Russ Conway. *Star Pics*

David Jacobs

127

1956 THE NORMAN WISDOM SHOW produced by Ernest Maxim under THE SATURDAY COMEDY HOUR banner. It starred Norman the ever popular comedian in various scenes with Marion Keene, Eddie Leslie and the George Mitchell singers.

1955-84 CRACKERJACK with master of ceremonies, Eamonn Andrews and produced by Johnny Downes, ran for nearly thirty years. Many artistes were involved including 'Mr Pastry', Leslie Crowther, Peter Glaze. June Whitfield made her first television appearance on it. A coveted prize in the Double or Drop Quiz was the Crackerjack pencil.

Drama programmes remained popular and of a high standard.

1957-8 TELEVISION WORLD THEATRE series included Classics like 'The Cherry Orchard' and gave Tony Hancock his first straight role as 'The Government Inspector' by Nikolai Gogul on 9.2.58. The following week:-

1958-61 SATURDAY PLAYHOUSE presented the 1933 Gaumont British hit 'Britannia of Billingsgate' with Hermione Baddeley in the leading role.

1957 SCHOOLS BROADCASTS began with 'Living with the Commonwealth'.

Another milestone was:-

16.10.1958 BLUE PETER Series Editor was 'Biddy' Baxter.

This programme has been the longest running magazine programme for children. At first it was a 15 min programme and the first edition had a item on toy trains and a demonstration of mind reading. It was then presented by Christopher Trace and Leila Williams and produced in Studio E. It later became a half-hour programme and Leila was replaced by Valerie Singleton in 1962. More than a dozen other presenters have appeared since and numerous pets. The programme has raised a lot of money for charities and has become a household name. When it was at Lime Grove the Blue Peter office was in one of the adjoining houses which reputedly had formerly been the house of a local prostitute.

Popular music played a large part in programmes.

1949 COME DANCING was established the year the BBC bought Lime Grove and is still running. Some episodes were transmitted from Lime Grove although it has had many venues in ballrooms around the country. When Cliff Michelmore interviewed Field Marshall Montgomery he asked him which was his favourite television programme and Montgomery replied, *Oh the one with all those pwetty girls in pwetty frocks.*

Many dance bands were featured as part of a show and some had their own:-

1956 WAKEY, WAKEY! produced by Brian Tesler featured the Billy Cotton Band and it's stars, so did:-

1956 THE TIN PAN ALLEY SHOW where the same band was conducted by Stanley Black.

1956 THE BILLY COTTON BAND SHOW was a 50 min variety show. It was a non stop song, dance and comedy show with Alan Breeze, Russ Conway and the exuberant Billy Cotton presenting and his son, Bill Cotton Jnr. producing. Bill Cotton Jnr. joined the BBC in 1956 and later became Head of Light Entertainment.

1957 THE EUROVISION SONG CONTEST The annual contest between competing European singers and groups for the best popular song of the year.

There were only ten countries competing in 1957, now there are twenty two. Katie Boyle hosted it for many years and Lime Grove hosted it sometimes in the early years.

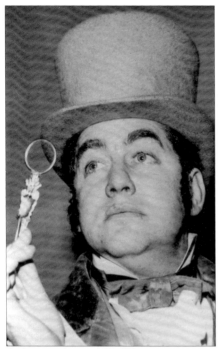

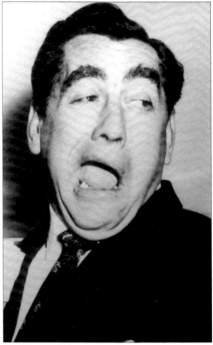

The Government Inspector 1958. BBC

Tony Hancock. BBC

Tony Hancock and Sid James. BBC

1957 THE ALMA COGAN SHOW In the late fifties and sixties, Alma Cogan was the first lady of popular music. She made guest appearances on many programmes, including, SUNDAY NIGHT AT THE LONDON PALLADIUM 1955-67. Her first appearance was in 1951 on THE YOUTH PARADE. RUNNING WILD 1954 featured the young Alma Cogan as resident singer on the first Morecombe & Wise show. She was known for her extravagant dresses and as 'the girl with the laugh in her voice'.

1959 JUKE BOX JURY was devised by Peter Potter and produced by Bill Cotton Jnr. The chairman was David Jacobs. In this programme a celebrity panel gave their verdict on the latest pop releases, and whether they thought they would be a hit or a miss. It was a weekly show and the first panel members were Alma Cogan; Pete Murray; Gary Miller and Susan Stranks, 'a typical teenager'. In a 1963 edition, The Beatles made up the jury. Katie Boyle was a regular panel guest.

1964 TOP OF THE POPS produced by Johnny Stewart. Presenters Jimmy Savile, Pete Murray, Alan Freeman and David Jacobs. The longest running British popular music show based on hits from the current weeks 'top twenty'. Some editions came from Studio G Lime Grove. It was advertised as a live show but viewers soon noticed the playing didn't always synchronise with the music and that in fact the players and singers were miming to recorded music. Some numbers were live, some recorded simply for acoustical reasons and lack of the original recording facilities in the TV studio.

These were the days when programmes were moving to White City and there were other BBC venues suitable for musical events but Lime Grove played its part. so many programmes from ANDY PANDY to HANCOCK'S HALF HOUR and DR. WHO, had their pilots and first series made at Lime Grove before moving on.

In 1954 the BBC bought Riverside Studios, a film studio built in 1933 on the river at Hammersmith. Also in 1954 they bought the Shepherd's Bush Empire, on the Green which was used for light entertainment shows when audience reaction was needed.

Ealing Studios were acquired in 1956.

General programme departments had all moved from Alexandra Palace to Lime Grove by 1953 with the exception of the Current Affairs, after 1956 Wood Lane began to be used. There was always a lot of 'toing and froing' of which it is difficult to keep track. NEWSNIGHT was moved from Wood Lane to Lime Grove in 1985, making an exception. News and current affairs was the last department to leave Alexandra Palace and it stayed at Lime Grove until the last, in 1991.

Although only for a short time Lime Grove was priviledged to be the home of:-

1956 HANCOCK'S HALF HOUR scripwriters were Ray Galton and Alan Simpson.

Tony Hancock was the comic genius of the fifties. He commented on things with which people could relate. When he said, *stone me what a life!* his audience agreed. They loved the way he took on bureaucracy, he didn't change it, but he tried. Tony Hancock had had success with his radio series and the show translated well into television. He had the perfect face for it and he had the perfect foil in Sid James. Hancock was a *yearning and pretentious striver, Sid his low and dodgy deflator.* There was a changing backup of other quality performers, Kenneth Williams, Hattie Jacques, Bill Kerr, Patricia Hayes, Irene Handl, Warren Mitchell and June Whitfield. Only the first series of six episodes was done at Lime Grove in Studio G.

Dixon of Dock Green 1955-76. Jack Warner

Z Cars 1962-78. Stratford Johns as Det. Chief Insp. Barlow. BBC

Z Cars. James Ellis as Insp. Lynch. BBC

Brian Blessed as P.C. Fancy Smith. BBC

It was a long, narrow studio, so that the audience was spread out along the longer dimension, four rows deep and about ninety feet long. The sets were similarly strung out, and the cameras had to work perpetually at an angle because they couldn't get back far enough from the cast to do head-on shots. It was a relief to everybody when they moved to Riverside Studios for the second and subsequent series – apart from anything else, the floors were smooth. At Lime Grove a camera tracking around on the floor was liable to look as if it was suffering from a minor earthquake. Roger Wilmutt 'Artiste'

The first series of six programmes started on 6.7.1956 and ended on 14.9.1956 but the whole series continued until 9.6.1961. The last three series of six episodes were pre-recorded, so they are the ones most people are familiar with. It is regrettable that more weren't recorded for posterity.

The first American 'Amplex' machine for telerecording was installed at Lime Grove on 1.10.1958 closely followed by another the following January and a further two by September 1959.

1956 Jack Warner in his autobiography tells how he was rehearsing Dixon of Dock Green at Sulgrave Boys Club, Goldhawk Road at the same time as Hancock's Half Hour was being rehearsed there in a different part of the building. Jack Warner says, *I tried my damndest to banish his frequent moods of gloom but met with little success. I told him how good Hancock's Half Hour was and asked him 'why should you worry'. 'I don't know, I suppose I'm just made like that',* Tony Hancock sadly replied. It was unfortunate for him that he was, he strove and was never satisfied with himself or his performance. Whilst working on a new television series in Australia in 1968 he committed suicide at only forty four, leaving us such a heritage of humour but how his loyal fans wished there had been more.

Jack Warner seemed to be playing out his role above as the fatherly confidant. The sort of character he played in:-

1955-76 DIXON OF DOCK GREEN The character of George Dixon first appeared in a film The Blue Lamp made at Ealing in 1949 by Michael Balcon. Ted Willis first wrote the script when prompted by Sydney Box and Gainsborough's script editor, Jan Read. The film was to have been made by Gainsborough but when that collapsed it passed to Ealing Films. Ted Willis kept the rights to the character George Dixon. Whilst having a drink in the BBC Club with Ronnie Waldman Ted Willis was asked if he could come up with a police series. Although in the film PC Dixon was shot by Dirk Bogarde, he was revived for a series which ran for twenty one years and was the first of many police dramas.

Jack Warner played a kindly East End policeman with a cosy family background. In each of the 36 episodes he greeted his viewers with *Evening All*. The early series rehearsed at Sulgrave Road Boys Club were made at Lime Grove and Riverside Studios. After the initial series of six, 30 min episodes, it was expanded to a further series of 45 min episodes and two tele-films. By the fifth series there was an audience of 14,000,000. George Dixon was finally promoted to Sergeant in 1964. Towards the end of the series there was a little more action and the viewers increased to 15,000,000. Local settings were used and one night George Dixon was on point duty at Notting Hill Gate when a distressed young girl rushed up to him and said she was being followed. Luckily a 'real' policeman was on hand to sort things out.

From 'Dixon' evolved a very authentic, tougher police drama series.

Steptoe and Son. Harry H. Corbett and Wilfred Brambell. Assoc. London Films

Dr. Findlay's Casebook. Andrew Cruikshank as Dr. Cameron.

Katie Boyle

1962-78 Z CARS produced by David E. Rose and written by Troy Kennedy Martin. Stratford Johns appeared as Detective Inspector Barlow. The series appeared twice weekly and was set in the Newtown estate in the north of England. It was altogether racier than Dixon and in its 50 min programmes it sometimes had 250 changes of shot. It reached *the peak of live television professionalism.* After the first eight programmes it had 14,000,000 viewers. No longer the fatherly coppers on the beat these policemen were human with all the consequent faults. Rehearsals, in this case, took place in the church hall of St. Luke's church, on the Uxbridge Road where the Shepherd's Bush Local History Society meet. There were two spin offs from this show, using the same characters, SOFTLY, SOFTLY 1971-73 and BARLOW AT LARGE 1974-5.

Z CARS had a memorable signature tune, 'Johnny Todd' played on Liverpool flutes and drums.

1962-65 STEPTOE AND SON with Wilfred Brambell and Harry H. Corbett and scripts by Ray Galton and Alan Simpson.

Like Hancock's Half Hour this programme went on through many series which when they are revived are as popular as ever.

Albert and Harold were Shepherd's Bush characters. Wood Lane was the home of 'totters' yards before it became the home of Television Centre and all the BBC satelites. The totters traversed the streets daily with their ponies and carts collecting junk and scrap. For the pilot a horse and cart were borrowed from a Wood Lane yard. St. Lukes church hall was used for rehearsals.

This series revolved around the relationship between Albert and Harold. Albert the father employed all his wiles to keep Harold's rebelious nature in check. Harold like Tony Hancock's character was always trying to better himself. Harold wanted to have wider interests, to improve his surroundings, perhaps to marry, even to move away and see the world. Albert always managed to bring their lives back to the status quo, living in their run down junk filled house with their run down junk filled yard which also housed, Hercules the horse and the kazi.

The series reached an outstanding viewing figure of 28,000,000 and was sold to the USA. There were originally twenty six 30 min episodes and further series in 1970, 1972 and 1974.

1962-71 DR. FINDLAY'S CASEBOOK was based on A.J. Cronin's story of a doctor's practice in a small Scottish town, Tannochbrae. It starred Andrew Cruikshank as Dr. Cameron, Bill Simpson as Dr. Findlay and Barbara Mullen as Janet, their housekeeper. It became a firm favourite and has been revived and the story continued in 1993 with Ian Bannen, David Rintoul, and Annette Crosbie. There were originally thirteen series of 200 30 min episodes.

Since that early boat race transmission of 1950, sports always formed a large slice of the programmes at Lime Grove. Cliff Michelmore's roving reporting led to the establishment of an early sports programme,

1954-68 SPORTSVIEW which was presented by Peter Dimmock. The first edition came out of Studio G and the teleprompter was used for the first time. This enables the reader to address the viewer whilst reading his script. A great improvement on crib cards. This programme showed Roger Bannister's four minute mile on May 6th 1954; The Piri-Zatopek duel at the White City; and the Olympic Games at Melbourne in 1956. An exhibition bout was given in the studio by Floyd Patterson World Heavyweight Champion. The programme had its own helicopter which sent radio pictures back to Lime Grove.

Frank Bough

Desmond Lynam

David Frost. London Weekend Television

Melvyn Bragg. London Weekend Television

135

1956-61 and 1964 SPORTS SPECIAL reported highlights of the weekend's sporting events. It was presented by Cliff Michelmore, David Coleman and Kenneth Wolstenholme. The first edition came out of Studio D.

There was even a sports programme for children.

1957-62 JUNIOR SPORTSVIEW it was introduced by Cliff Michelmore and presented by Danny Blanchflower and Billy Wright, two famous footballers.

1958-82 GRANDSTAND is the world's longest running live sports series and on Saturday afternoons it presents a five hour non-stop sports service. David Coleman became the regular presenter and link man until he felt he wanted *to get out more to shake off the yellow pallor brought on by the lights of Studio E, Lime Grove.*

1968 it was then that Frank Bough took over. In his book "Cue Frank!" he describes graphically what it was like to be a link man and having the combined voices of all the outside broadcast reports relayed to you in the studio. All the commentators were linked to Studio E via their 'hearing aids' and the producer, Martin Hopkins, would be directing the cameras and co-ordinating all their material. *Mission Control with vengence*, said Frank. In turn they were linked with Television Centre in Wood Lane where the videotaping was done. Even though technology had advanced since the early fifties boat race it was still a nightmare. The number of cameras at a big event like the boat race Frank called *a television jigsaw puzzle. Even on a normal Saturday all the live and film events had to be co-ordinated with the teletector slides of famous players; countdown to the videotape clips of goals; dealing with postponements, delays and changes of programme. Having to transfer to basketball from football just when things were getting exciting. Rushing around the country from game to game and keeping the whole thing as a whole.* The finished transmissions were what the viewers wanted for GRANDSTAND continues today.

1965 SUNDAY CRICKET was produced by Alan Mouncer, and presented by Frank Bough. In the sixties sports programmes on Sunday were not acceptable but by organising Sunday charity cricket matches the idea was made more palatable. Top class players from all over the world were gathered together. *The International Cavaliers* as they were known, played *The Counties.* The programme made cricket popular with viewers.

John Arlott did commentories and Frank Bough interviewed famous players.

1981 SUNDAY GRANDSTAND began on BBC2.

Another great television personality was Huw Wheldon who joined the BBC as a Publicity Officer but soon moved on to become a presenter, first in children's television, in:-

1954 ALL YOUR OWN produced by Cliff Michelmore.

He introduced talented children and their hobbies. A pianist was needed and Violet Carson joined the programme as an accompaniest. She was later to find fame in Coronation Street as Ena Sharples. Many of the young entrants went on to find fame in their sphere. The most famous of all was Jacqueline du Pré who charmed everyone on the set. Huw Weldon, with his striking looks, large nose and brilliant eyes, played the part of an 'enthusiastic uncle' well and his young competitors liked him. He had presented childrens programmes earlier, CHILDREN'S NEWSREEL 1950 and IT'S ALL YOURS. He was enthusiastic from the beginning, *I am now in this television thing which is a jungle*, he said. He was paid 15 guineas for each appearance in addition to his salary as Publicity Officer. He produced:-

That Was The Week That Was 1962. David Frost, Roy Kinnair, Kenneth Cope, Lance Percival, William Rushton. BBC

That Was The Week That Was 1962. Millicent Martin. BBC

1956-7 MEN IN BATTLE with Sir Brian Horrocks, who spoke of the great battles of the Second World War. Whilst in the studio Sir Brian insisted in giving all the technicians army ranks and addressing them by it. Huw Wheldon produced many programmes in a military vein after joining "Talks", including:-

Jan 29 1956 FOR VALOUR to celebrate the centenary of the Victoria Cross and PORTRAITS OF POWER. Finally he found his true niche in the arts, he produced:-

1955 PRESS CONFERENCE with various guests, one was with Orson Welles. He said of Orson Welles, *He was one of the most remarkable people I have ever met and I didn't feel the programme did him justice.* Huw Weldon then produced a series, ORSON WELLES SKETCHBOOK 1955.

1958-65 MONITOR was hosted by Huw Weldon.

This was the first regular arts programme in British television and possibly the world, said Ken Russell. It introduced Ken Russell, Melvyn Bragg, Jonathan Miller, Humphrey Burton and John Schlesinger to the general public. Huw Weldon had absolute control in his editorship and created something unique. Just as well he was given a free hand as he called Grace Wyndham Goldie *a clever tyrant* and wouldn't have taken any direction from above.

The programme is best remembered for its biographies, mainly involving Ken Russell; Elgar 1962; Debussy 1965; Rousseau 1965; Cranks at Work 1960; The Miner's Picnic; Shelagh Delaney's Salford, Prokofiev; Bela Bartok 1964; Rossetti; Richard Strauss and Mahler. John Schlesinger produced his Circus 1958; Benjamin Britten; Innocent Eye and The Class, the list is extensive and remarkable.

Both Ken Russell and John Schlesinger went on to become feature film directors and to international fame and Melvyn Bragg to produce his own arts programme. The programme appeared twice monthly and Huw Wheldon with his studied relaxation was the perfect host. In the first year of the programme alone, there appeared on the show, Kingsley Amis, John Bratby, Sir Jacob Epstein, Yehudi Menuhin, Charles Laughton, Michael Ayrton, Leonie Massine, Aldous Huxley, Tyrone Guthrie, Duke Ellington, P.G. Woodhouse, Aaron Copeland, William Alwyn, Peter Brook, E.M. Forster and Georges Simeon, filmed in Switzerland by John Schlesinger. Also Maria Callas, whom Humphrey Burton was told, *to look after,* a daunting task. A fuss was made that she was an hour making up, but with the final effect being so stunning it doesn't seem excessive.

MONITOR made Huw Wheldon a great name, deservedly as he contributed a lot to the programme.

Another outstanding programme was:-

1959 FACE TO FACE presented by John Freeman and produced by Hugh Burnett. It was a searching interview programme at first of 15 mins and then 30 mins. Interviewees included Dame Edith Sitwell, 6.5.69; Professor Carl Jung, 22.11.59; Tony Hancock, 7.2.60; Gilbert Harding, 18.9.60; Adam Faith, 11.12.60 and Dr. Martin Luther King 29.10.61. What a list! Felix Topolski often did caricatures of the subjects for the opening and closing sequences.

An innovative and memorable programme of the time was:-

1962-63 THAT WAS THE WEEK THAT WAS

It was a satire on the week's news produced by David Frost and his team, Roy Kinnear, Lance Percival, Kenneth Cope, Eleanor Bron, William Rushton, Bernard Levin, Al Mancini, singers

John Schlesinger

Ken Russell

The Daleks

William Hartnell

David Kernan and Millicent Martin, and cartoonist Timothy Birdsall. Ned Sherrin produced the 30 min show. *There was a new degree of honesty on racism, religion, patriotism, and politicians, it was never out of the headlines.* Peter Blake.

The show was so topical it was only put together on Saturday to be shown Saturday night. It was shown in a skilfully casual way with cameras and booms in shot.

Other series followed but none had the impact of this one. It caused controversy with everyone, including the BBC, from the beginning and became the most talked about television programme in the world.

A Canadian, Sydney Newman moved to the BBC from ITV to become Head of the Drama Group. The brief he was given was to fill a spot in the early evening programme, after SATURDAY SPORT to keep the ratings up. He came up with:-

23.9.1963 DR. WHO who was 720 years old, was lost in outer space and had a time machine which he was not sure how to work. Consequently he and his passengers never quite knew where they would land when next trying to return to earth. The pilot "An Unearthly Child" took just one day and a budget of £2,000 to make. Verity Lambert, production assistant chose William Hartnell for the first Doctor. It was decided not to aim at just children but the whole family *Intelligent children and childlike adults.* The haunting signature tune was created by Ron Grainer from pre-recorded notes copied at various speeds, unusual then. On October 18th 1963, the revised pilot was shot in Studio D, Lime Grove. Taking 45 mins from the unusual opening credits to the end. This was shown as the first episode, followed by the contracted fifty two episodes. The first episode went out 10 minutes late as President Kennedy's assassination the previous day had caused so much extra news. It went out at 5.15 pm on Saturday November 23rd and again on the following Saturday.

The second episode contained THE DALEKS. Designers Raymond Cusick and Jack King were given a budget of £700 for them. The first one was put together at Wood Lane where many of the workshops had moved. Only four could be produced within this budget so the other two were enlarged photographic copies. Each one had an actor inside, sitting on a stool. During Lime Grove tea breaks they were often forgotten and left inside. The flashing lights were indicator lights from an old Morris 8. The Daleks were used with misgiving but the 8,000,000 viewers loved them. Although destroyed in the episode they had to be ressurrected for further instalments. Every child could identify with a Dalek and their awful cry, *Exterminate, exterminate!*

The second year found the programme with 10,000,000 fans and it continued for twenty one years until 1984. It was shown in Australia, Canada and the USA and has become a cult.

Cliff Michelmore said, *Lime Grove was where you had to be if you wanted to be part of this expanding and exciting service. I was at Lime Grove most of the time meeting other producers in canteens at lunchtime or at THE WHITE HORSE or THE BRITISH PRINCE in the early evenings. These pubs were at either end of Lime Grove. At the Prince you would find childrens producers and some from drama. Turn right and at the White Horse you would find the 'young turks' of the talks department, together with the sports crowd.*

The whole of this area of Shepherd's Bush was taken over by the studios. Even the portions in the RITZ restaurant in Goldhawk Road were for electricians and sceneshifters appetites. The local economy must have suffered when the BBC finally moved to Wood Lane. Half of The White Horse is now a video hire store in 1996. Forty years back Cliff Michelmore could

Alan Whicker. BBC

Peter Snow

Sue Lawley

Peter Sissons

already have spent the day working at Playbox, All Your Own, Children's Sport, Real Adventure, Saturday Sport and Panorama before preparing for Highlight that evening. Donald Baverstock's office was in the backroom of a terrace house and it was there the maxim *we should be asking the questions viewers would ask if they had thought of them* was made. There were usually three interviewees but if one failed to reach Shepherd's Bush or the studio the others were stretched to fill the ten minutes. Once, only one arrived and he had to fill the whole programme, a champion hamslicer. Every type of person was interviewed from heads of state to the man in the street who had realised his moment of fame. Louis Armstrong was the interviewee Cliff Michelmore most liked. Politics, sport, the arts, or international affairs were all covered. Broadcasting House was ruffled by the new style.

Feb. 1957-65 TONIGHT with a programme time of 45 min, appeared five nights a week, at 6.00 pm. It was an extended Highlight which ran for eight years and 1,800 editions. It recruited personalities like Fyffe Robertson, Trevor Philpot, Alan Whicker, MacDonald Hastings, John Morgan, Polly Elwes (the first woman reporter), Derek Hart, Geoffrey Johnson-Smith, Julian Pettifer, Kenneth Allsop, Brian Redhead and Magnus Magnusson. Alan Whicker made his television debut here and he and many of the others went on to have their own programmes and Tonight was the forerunner for programmes like Whicker's World and That Was The Week That Was.

Alan Whicker said, *we had to be prepared to try our hand at everything it was very exciting.* Cliff Michelmore said, *we brought the world to Lime Grove to enlighten, entertain and excite.* He interviewed Sir Matt Busby; Bob Hope; Nubar Gulbenkian; Mike Todd, who came so often they named a set after him; Dame Edith Sitwell; Yehudi Menuhin; Flanders and Swann; and Gene Kelly who persuaded Cliff Michelmore to make a dancing entrance with him down long narrow Studio E. Bernard Levin produced topical calypsos for the programme. Idi Amin was interviewed for it by David Lomax, who had been expelled from Uganda previously. Idi Amin asked him, *Are you not afraid of interviewing the conqueror of the British empire?* Undeterred Lomax asked him, *Why is it so many prominent people in his country disappear?* Alan Whicker began his roving reports. Live broadcasts from all over the world were included and co-ordinated in the studio. The picture journalism was shot by the best cameramen.

TONIGHT was *classless, colloquial, friendly and irreverent.* It had 8,000,000 viewers. Cliff Michelmore was there from the beginning to the end. On one occasion in a power cut, Ned Sherrin remembers being interviewed by him on a fire escape with the Metropolitan trains rattling by in the background. On another occasion when the lift stuck, Cliff Michelmore introduced TONIGHT from inside it. The signature tune was 'Tonight and Everynight' and Cliff Michelmore ended with *And the next Tonight is tomorrow night.*

The pet shop in Shepherd's Bush Market maintained the fish tank which appeared behind the credits on the Tonight programme until one night it broke and Cliff was only able to display one surviving fish on the next evening's programme. Probably it was the same pet shop who supplied the rats for 1984. David Stone from the Cable department said, *the sounds of Shepherd's Bush Market as heard from the Studios was reminiscent of the Casbah in Marrakesh.*

The Daleks paid a visit to the market at Christmas 1963 and it was a happy hunting ground for programmes like Thats Life!

Michael Barratt

Gloria Hunniford, Gloria Live 1990. Thames Television

Esther Ranzen, That's Life 1973

Russell Grant. Jacque Evans

In 1965 the TONIGHT team were transferred to:-
1965-72 TWENTY FOUR HOURS which was a magazine programme that went out at 10.30 pm looking back on the world events of the day.

Continuing with current affairs programmes through the years:-
1964-84 NATIONWIDE was a popular current affairs programme created by Derrick Amoore. It went out early evening where formerly Tonight had been. Michael Barratt and Frank Bough were the presenters. Frank Bough interviewed Bing Crosy for it at the Paladium. It was his last interview as he collapsed and died on the golf course four days later.

The Nationwide office was like a penthouse on the roof of the main block. It was complete chaos inside with last minute amendments to the show and more swearing than in any army barracks.

1967 Limited colour service began in July with five hours a day as an experiment but in December it was increased to thirty hours, colour had arrived. Studios D and E at Lime Grove were converted to colour, 625 lines.

1975 TONIGHT was revived with Sue Lawley, Denis Tuomy and Donald MacCormick as co-presenters. Sue Lawley spent eleven years at Lime Grove working on NATIONWIDE and TONIGHT. She says she,

Won't forget how much walking I had to do, the Nationwide office was on the seventh floor, our studio was on the fourth floor and to get to the canteen you had to go down to the first floor, through a scene dock and then across a fire escape. However she also says, *The building has always been a home to me and when people criticise it, it makes my hackles rise but admittedly it was actually quite dreary and... a terribly difficult place to work.*

1979 QUESTION TIME a 60 min programme chaired for the first ten years by Sir Robin Day. A panel of four politicians were asked questions of the moment by a studio audience. Robin Day's probing caused a few affronts but he was a masterly interviewer. Peter Sissons took over in 1989.

4.6.1984 SIXTY MINUTES a current affairs programme which replaced NATIONWIDE. When its closure was announced, the technicians protested by blacking it out. It became:-

1985 NEWSNIGHT which had the distinction of moving from Wood Lane to Lime Grove in 1985. The presenters were Peter Snow, Peter Hobday, Charles Wheeler, John Tusa and Fran Morrison. Sports news came from David Davies. It was the first time the BBC combined its news and current affairs departments to produce an in-depth news programme at the end of the day, featuring interviews and debate on the days news.

Two years earlier a programme was started to interest viewers at the beginning of the day,

1983 BREAKFAST TIME on January 17th Britain and Europe's first breakfast television began. It had a lightweight, attractive and informal team, led by Frank Bough, the link people were Selena Scott, and Nick Ross. Joined by Debbie Rix, newsreader; David Icke, sportscaster; Diana Moran, keep fit; Russell Grant, astrologer; Chris Wilson, gossip columnist; Glynn Christian, cookery expert and Francis Wilson a weatherman with sex appeal. Mike Smith and Fern Britton also appeared. The programme editor was Ron Neil. Frank Bough arrived at the studio each morning at 4.00 am for transmission at 6.30 am. The informal atmosphere was copied from shows in the States. It was a success and Channel 3 soon followed with a suitably sparkling line-up on TV-AM.

Demolition of Lime Grove Studios. David Stone

145

Russell Grant is a member of the Shepherd's Bush Local History Society. He said on joining, *I lived in Askew Road for over seven years in the 1970s. It is an area of great importance to my own personal heritage as my grandparents owned the triangular fish and chip shop in St. Elmo Road, back in the 1930s. My mother worked at the old Gainsborough Studios in the 1940s and my own career took off at BBC Lime Grove now sadly closed.*

When almost all but current affairs and news programmes had moved to Wood Lane, White City there were still some feature programmes produced at Lime Grove, such as:-

1973-94 THAT'S LIFE! Presented by Esther Ranzen and her team. It was a consumer watchdog series at the man-on-the-street level with investigations into public and private services. Readers could send in their experiences of bad service and they would be investigated with zeal and humour. The programme had a great effect and much permanent good was done and money raised for good causes.

1987 KILROY with Robert Kilroy-Silk discussing topics of the day directly with and amongst the studio audience. The audience gathered before the show in the Gainsborough Suite. Many lables from earlier days remained until the end.

1990 GLORIA LIVE and **GLORIA** with Gloria Hunniford discussing issues of the day in the studio with guests and the audience. A morning show, Monday to Friday, produced by Jill Dawson.

1990 WATCHDOG with Lynn Faulds Wood was another consumer watchdog series on products rather than services. Again much good was done and faulty products exposed.

1990-91 THE LATE SHOW was an arts programme with a magazine format. This programme was appropriately the last transmisson from Lime Grove in June 1991. The music of the late show faded, the endless corridors were empty, the fire escapes no longer rattled as late comers tried to find their way, everyone had moved to Television Centre. An attempt to interest English Heritage in preserving Lime Grove as a momument to the film and television industry failed and the fantasy factory was demolished in September 1993.

David Stone who worked at Lime Grove for twenty five years, watched and photographed the demolition. He says,

During the actual demolition I witnessed a chap standing on the large metal ball, used on the crane for knocking down the walls. He was hoisted up in the air holding the cable in one hand and an oxyacetylene torch in the other. He climbed onto one of the large R.S.J. iron supports, 80' up and cut three quarters through it before casually climbing back onto the ball to be lowered to the ground. The crane driver hit the girder with the ball and down it crashed causing much dust and dismay to all the local pigeons! Lime Grove was always the home for thousands of pigeons. The lorries carried the tons of rubble away to become the foundations for the M25 Motorway widening scheme. The frontage on Lime Grove was the last bit to be demolished.

1995 houses were built for the Notting Hill Housing Trust and the former history of the site is perpetuated in their names, 'Gainsborough Court' and 'Gaumont Terrace'. In 1987 an over enthusiastic BBC producer described the building as, *a dark and dismal tenement, a grimey rat-infested warren* but most people only have warm memories of Lime Grove. Cliff Michelmore said, *all buildings are made by the people inside them and at its height Lime Grove was full of the most extraordinary people you could ever hope to meet.*

Humphrey Burton said, *we were very lucky. Everyone who worked there in that period agrees, that it was a truly golden age. It will never be the same again as it was at Lime Grove. They were the happiest days of my life.*

The BBC Television Centre 1960. A.J. Howard

BIBLIOGRAPHY

The World Film Encyclopedia, Edited Clarence Winchester. Amalgamated Press 1933
Film Pictorial Christmas Annual, Edited Clarence Winchester. 1933
The Picture Show Annual, Amalgamated Press 1934
20 Years Of British Film, Michael Balcon and others. Falcon Press 1947
Richard Dimbleby Broadcaster, Edited by Leonard Miall. BBC 1966
The History Of The British Film 1918-1929, Rachel Low. Allen & Unwin 1971
The Biggest Aspidestra In The World, Peter Black. BBC 1972
Jessie Matthews, Michael Thornton. Hart-Davis MacGibbon 1974
Jack Of All Trades, Jack Warner. W.H.Allen 1975
Hitch, John Russell Taylor. Faber and Faber 1978
Artiste – Tony Hancock, Roger Wilmut. Eyre Methuen 1978
Up In The Clouds Gentlemen Please, John Mills. Weidenfelt & Nicholson 1980
Cue Frank, Frank Bough. Queen Anne Press 1980
Before I Forget, James Mason. Sphere Books 1981
Isobel Barnet, Jock Callager. Methuen 1982
British Sound Films – The Studio Years 1928-1959, David Quinland. 1984
Dr Who – 21st Anniversary Book, Peter Haining. 1984
Coming To You Live, narrated by Denis Norden. Methuen 1985
A Life In The Movies, Michael Powell. Methuen 1986
Uninvited Guests, Laurie Taylor and Bob Mullan. Chatto & Windus 1986
Two Way Story, Cliff Michelmore & Jean Metlalfe. Hamish Hamilton 1986
Peter Cushing An Autobiography. Weidenfelt & Nicholson 1986
The Best Of British, Maurice Sellar and others. Sphere Books 1987
Eamonn Andrews His Life, Gus Smith. W.H. Allen 1988
Eamonn Andrews, Tom Brennand. Weidenfeld & Nicholson 1989
The Man Between – A Biography Of Carol Reed, Nicholas Wapshott. Chatto & Windus 1990
Sir Hugh – Life Of Huw Weldon, Paul Ferris. Michael Joseph 1990
Evening All, Ted Willis. Macmillan 1991
John Mills, Robert Tanitch. Collins Brown 1993
Fire Over England, Ken Russell. Hutchinson 1993
Halliwells Film Guide, Edited by John Walker. Harper Collins 1993
Britsh Television, Tise Vahimagi. Oxford University Press 1994
The Evening Standard. The Star. The London Evening News.
The West London Observer. Radio Times. Ariel.
The Listener & John Gau. The Spectator. The Independant.
Tony Hancock Society Publications.

INDEX OF NAMES

INDEX OF TITLES

PHOTOGRAPHS

Photographs by courtesy of:-

The British Film Institute Stills Library
1, 6, 7, 9, 10, 12, 13, 14, 19, 22, 25-30,
34-38, 41, 42, 43, 45, 47-54, 56-61, 67,
71, 75-83, 85, 86, 87, 90-95, 107-113,
115-121, 125-133, 138, 140, 141,
145-152, 154-159, 233 & 234

Audrey Atterbury
165-168

BBC Picture Archives Photograph Library
210

Dave Sandall, Tony Hancock Society
219-221

Russell Grant
246

David Stone
247, 248

The remainder of the photographs
Ventafile
14 Keith Grove, London W12 9EZ